Marketing

in

Commercial Property

by

Martin Newman

With a Foreword by

Christopher Jonas CBE FRICS

1997

lon W1V 4BN

ess Information

First published 1997

ISBN 0 7282 0277 8

Printed in Great Britain by The Lavenham Press Ltd, Suffolk

Acknowledgements

1989 was not the most propitious time to enter the commercial property sector and yet, for all the challenges and pain of the intervening years, it has never been less than a lively and friendly working environment. For this I have to thank my colleagues in Healey & Baker, those marketing professionals in competing firms, the property media, colleagues in the Professional Services Marketing Group, and the many skilled agencies and suppliers with whom I have worked.

Some of these people have been kind enough to contribute the case studies that add substance to the thoughts expressed:
Anne-Marie Stebbings of lawyers Simmons & Simmons; *Stewart Jones* of EGi;
Sophie Rush of Knight Frank; *Michel Pilette* of Jones Lang Wootton;
Ali Ballantyne of Nelson Bakewell; *Mike Mulholland* of Quest Design;
Patrick Going of Healey & Baker; *Roger Lister* of Richard Ellis;
Alvaro Portela and *Cristina Candido* of Sonae Imobiliária; and
John Rushton of The Small Back Room.
I am indebted too to research consultant, *Karen Randolph* and to *Frank Hore* of
The Service Marketing Partnership for their contributions.

A special vote of thanks to *James Hollington* of Healey & Baker who
patiently read through the text in its raw state, and gave the most constructive advice
to correct here and suggest there from his own wealth of experience in the UK and
continental property sector. Any remaining failings are the author's alone.

The physical production of the book is
the result of the support and hard work of colleagues –
Margaret Millar in typing the document and *Paul O'Flynn* in designing the layout.

Thanks are due to my wife *Jennifer* who, as my fiercest critic, encouraged me in the
project from first to last, and shared in the lost evenings and weekends.

The book is written very much in the hope that it will encourage still further
the development of marketing in commercial property. For that reason,
it is hopefully unstuffy, short on academic theory and, above all, practical.

Lastly, I am grateful to the staff of the *Estates Gazette* for their support and
encouragement during the preparation of this book.

Foreword by
Christopher Jonas CBE FRICS

It may seem strange that there should be a need for a new book on marketing in the commercial property market. After all most people in property make their living by buying or selling it. People should be pretty skilled by now.

But on reflection it is not so strange. For as long as most of us can remember property has effectively sold itself. The market seemed to rise almost as of right and every instruction would turn into a fee. Similarly the demand for property professionals was very strong for years.

All that has now long since changed. Property has to be sold with real skill in order to achieve a deal. There are too many advisory firms around so it is imperative to know how to market oneself and to differentiate ones services from the herd.

Accordingly Mr. Newman's book seems well timed. And an excellent digest of current thinking in this subject area. No theory or written material can ever substitute for the inspiration which lands that sale or instruction. Or the broad range of personal contacts which have always been so important for success in the property markets. But there is a strong case for having read the best that there is on the subject. It makes one think and also ensures we are abreast with the best ideas.

Marketing in Commercial Property is just that volume. The wise will use part of their spare time in 1997 to read it. And to reflect on whether it can suggest just one extra edge that they use in their presentation of themselves or their clients' property.

Contents Page no.

List of Figures

List of Illustrations

Chapter 1

Introduction

It is 13 years since the Estates Gazette first published a book on marketing. Edward Cleaveley's *"The Marketing of Industrial and Commercial Property"*[1] proved to be a valuable and popular book at a time when marketing, as a formal discipline, was only just appearing within the industry. It was described as the impending revolution! Indeed, the cover notes of that book said that marketing "will inevitably dominate the letting of industrial and commercial property over the next decade".

We all know now of course that the decade in question saw boom followed by bust – not only in the letting market but across other areas of commercial property activity. It is often said that the property industry is a good barometer for the economy in general and that its performance is dictated by the general business climate. Whilst accepting the relationship, there can be little doubt that some of the pain felt in the property industry in the 1990s could have been avoided. In practice, marketing was too often carried out badly or not practised at all for there to have been so many failures – of organisations and projects – over the last few years.

Has marketing arrived?

On a more positive note, marketing has made some very real progress in the last 13 years. The marketing of properties is altogether more sophisticated and impressive now, bearing out Edward Cleaveley's prediction. This is covered in Section II of this book. Where there remains room for improvement is in corporate marketing – the marketing of companies and their services. For this reason the first, and greater, part of this book is given over to that.

In general, most players in the sector do carry out marketing activities much more professionally now than then. And in terms of adopting a marketing approach to business there have been increasing signs over the last couple of years that organisations are now questioning their strategy and resource allocation much more closely. More individuals are better trained and more aware of the marketing concept than previously, and there has been some reallocation of resources.

This is genuinely revolutionary and, though most firms claim to be client centred, not enough have followed through the (marketing) implications of that. Even after the market of the last five years, the penny has still not dropped with some. Though marketing cannot avoid the impact of broader economic activity, it can help organisations take better advantage of upturns and protect themselves more in hostile markets. Marketing is about risk reduction as much as creating opportunities, and this at last is being recognised.

This book examines afresh what marketing is and how it might be practised within the property sector. It is inevitably a practical book, since marketing is rooted in real market behaviour rather than theory. I have deliberately not sought to write a general purpose marketing textbook since enough of these exist already. Rather I have attempted to concentrate on what is applicable to the sector, and to express it in as straightforward a manner as possible.

Included in the text are examples of marketing initiatives contributed by a number of the best practitioners in the industry. The book should therefore be of interest to all those managing or aspiring to manage within the sector, as well as all those directly involved in marketing or business development.

There is, perhaps inevitably, an emphasis on the activities of surveyors since this is where most marketing practice in the sector tends to be concentrated.

It is difficult now to imagine that the industry can go on much longer without the marketing "revolution" taking a firmer hold. Already the more aware companies and firms have sorted out their basic strategic positioning in the market. Some have opted for a UK regional presence, some have concentrated on developing a European or global service, others have expanded their service range, while others have concentrated on specific market sectors.

Gone too is talk of market share, which in this industry is refreshing. Few sectors in the UK are as difficult to measure as commercial property. The very diffuse nature of the market, the unannounced deals, the secrecy surrounding some transactions all make it difficult to assess the full scale of the market. Notwithstanding this, such estimates that have been made within commercial surveying for example give, typically, a market share of around 5% only to the leaders with the top half dozen firms accounting collectively for less than a quarter of the market. At this level market share is meaningless corporately – you cannot start dictating to the market with only a 5% market share. Even so, the big firms do perhaps watch each other too closely. Reacting to market developments is one thing, but there is still a tendency to follow the herd even when it may not be commercially advantageous.

Reactive behaviour is both a strength and a sign of weakness. Throughout the 1980s firms learnt to react quickly and well, delivering a high level of service often at very short notice to the increasing level of instructions flooding the market. It was hard work but the rewards were high. Inevitably the opportunism and greed without considered evaluation of demand caused the market to overheat. Given the long lead time in development between market assessment and completion of the project, many were caught out. Speed of response when nobody is asking has limited value. Many surveying firms cut their staff numbers, some drastically. Other staff were switched into the professional service functions, where demand for work has been less volatile. Indeed it is the arguably less glamorous professional service functions that have helped some firms survive in the 1990s.

A feature of the reactive behaviour in the industry was the cutting of marketing staff and budgets. Few of those staff brought in in the 1980s survived. Budgets had been voted without proper assessment. They were cut back to levels that made one wonder whether firms knew why they were spending money in the first place. These budgets must have been wrong before, or they are wrong now since corporate needs have not moved dramatically. This smacks of marketing budgets being set at levels that could be "afforded" rather than at levels needed to deliver targeted performance – a self-fulfilling route to under-performance if ever there were one. This suggests that marketing is still not properly understood.

Improved marketing practices

In spite of the slow progress in the industry in adopting the marketing concept, some aspects have become much more sophisticated in their practice in recent years. Branding has received a lot of attention, and rightly so, as it is one way of differentiating from competitors. Most of the leading firms of surveyors have reviewed the market's perception of them and adjusted their branding accordingly (*see illustration on page 74-5*). Some of the visual changes have been marked, others minimal, and we will look at examples of each and why it was done in Chapter 6. A key element of branding too, which has been well recognised, is the need to communicate internally to staff as well as externally to clients.

The practice of "beauty" parades has become much more prevalent over the period, the more so as the public sector has been forced to demonstrate an objective process in selecting professional advisers and awarding contracts. One product of this is the improved quality of business pitches. Too often the brief is under prepared but firms spend considerable time and effort in responding now, not just in putting together *a* presentation, but in genuinely addressing the client's perceived needs. This extra thought, preparation and rehearsal, as well as enhanced materials and equipment, has led to an altogether higher standard of presentations (in fact, a higher standard than the professionalism or courtesy of some clients deserves!).

Just as the attention to client needs prior to winning the instruction has heightened, so client care throughout the relationship is given more attention. Having seen various service sectors in my working life, I have consistently been impressed by the attention paid to the professional service supplied to the client in the commercial property sector. (As an aside, I think this is also the strongest single argument for the partnership structure.) The extra competitive edge engendered by the market conditions of the 1990s, however, has led firms to redouble their efforts in looking after their more valued clients. We shall look in more detail at the whole area of business winning and retention in Chapter 5. Both require an element of intuitive skills, but, equally, these skills can be developed.

Training has always been accorded significant attention within the industry, but it has tended to focus on the necessary training of professional skills. Many firms offer genuine career development paths from graduate level to partner or director. For their own future prosperity they have long seen the benefits of devoting time and effort to developing professional competence. What is more recent, however, is the training of an altogether broader range of skills related not just to business winning and retention but also to the development of surveyors as businessmen. In Chapter 5 "Adapting" we shall look at the necessity of training, not just to produce people to run the business more competently, but also to better understand and advise clients.

The enhanced standards of performance within the sector are increasingly being recognised externally, with various awards being won within the sector. A number of firms have opted to apply for and gain such standards as BS5750 and ISO9000 which, although not a judgement on performance quality, at least verify that the procedures for continuous assessment are in place. This is probably most relevant within the professional service and corporate areas of activity, particularly where target clients are from the public sector.

The training and development of staff is also measurable by external, cross-industry standards. The Investors in People Award entails a process of rigorous external assessment by the Training and Enterprise Councils and examines commitment to staff training and development. Drivers Jonas and Healey & Baker have both received the Award.

Forces that have reshaped marketing in the sector

The biggest impact on marketing in the sector since the early 1980s has been the roller coaster of boom followed by bust. Each period in its own way saw heightened attention given to marketing activities.

The boom period of the 1980s saw development schemes of an unprecedented scale that tested the market's capabilities to absorb. Many were the result of public/private sector co-operation as the awareness bit that inward investment has to be competed for. This testing of the market prompted marketing promotion on a scale and of a quality not seen before, which served to raise standards across the sector.

The subsequent collapse in the market through the 1990s led to a fierce cutting back of marketing budgets, both for corporate and project promotion. The upshot has been that each pound spent is now rigorously vetted. This too has helped to ensure more disciplined expenditure and, if not more effective promotion, certainly more cost-effective promotion.

A further major change in the sector since Edward Cleaveley's book[1] has been the internationalisation of the market, both inward and outward. Investors, traders and, to a lesser extent developers have increasingly expanded their activities globally. Surveying firms have been quick to react, with all the leading firms seizing the opportunity to expand their work internationally. The concept of the professional surveyor was scarcely known outside the UK, opening the prospect of exporting an essentially British skill to compete with, largely broker, indigenous competitors.

This has been a genuine marketing success story: markets have been assessed for their potential; firms have adapted either organically or by association; and the service promoted. Some firms now generate close to half their fee income outside the UK. This success has recently been recognised by the Queen's Award for Export Achievement in 1996 to Healey & Baker. Such has been the strength of the service provided by firms that business has not just been obtained from British interests overseas but, more often, from local clients. In Healey & Baker's case, 80% typically of the business of an international office will be non-British. As Senior Partner Paul Orchard-Lisle said on receiving the Queen's Award: "Invisible earnings from commercial real estate has been one of the unsung success stories of the last ten years. UK firms have led the way..." (*see illustration on page 69*)

To bolster the position gained by the leading firms the Royal Institution of Chartered Surveyors has established an International Office and a network of representatives and correspondents worldwide. The European Society of Chartered Surveyors represents over 70,000 chartered surveyors throughout the European Union. Its aims are also: to facilitate training, qualification and mutual recognition; to establish Community-wide standards of professional practice and codes of conduct; and to support and promote development of the property and construction professions.

Postgraduate courses in Amsterdam and Frankfurt have already been approved and successful students can apply to become chartered surveyors, subject to completing two years of practical experience and the APC. A new pan-European profession is being created.

One of the comfort factors companies look for when trading internationally is knowledge about the market. For all the secrecy surrounding some individual transactions the weight of research in the sector, both internationally and within the UK, has grown both in quantity and quality. I stress here that I refer to research about property and its performance, not marketing research. The leading firms all have significant research functions delivering high-standard material in the form of privately commissioned studies as well as published reports. (*see illustration on page 70*)

Underpinning market knowledge is the intelligence database. This is hugely enhanced by the development of information technology within the sector, which is the other really significant change of the last 10 years. Moreover, I suspect "we ain't seen nothing yet" since although many firms now have installed a range of equipment and systems, their facility in using them to full advantage both for themselves and their clients is still developing.

There are now many more marketing professionals working in the sector. Most firms do now have at least one professionally qualified marketing person on board internally. Some are experienced marketing practitioners, bringing skills acquired in other areas to the sector.

Help from professional bodies

There are a number of external organisations that can help the development of marketing within commercial property. I would like to see the RICS giving more weight to marketing in its proper sense within the syllabus, rather than concentrating on those promotional activities that are mostly linked to agency work. Indeed, discussing promotion as marketing could encourage surveyors to a narrow view of marketing and hold back the adoption and development of marketing in the sector. Happily, the Institution has recently commissioned a RICS Marketing Education Tape, which does begin look at marketing on a somewhat broader basis.

Of considerable help is the Chartered Institute of Marketing, whose Diploma remains the benchmark qualification for all marketing people. Their programme of courses covers individual marketing skills to broad strategic management and will suit young practitioners to chief executives accordingly. In recent years, too, they have made a point of developing marketing courses for the service industries, recognising that the application of marketing to services is different from its application in the consumer products world.

Chapter 3 looks at some of the specific issues relating to marketing within the professional service environment. Largely because the challenge is special, a number of marketing practitioners within professional services set up, in 1989, the Professional Services Marketing Group. There are now over 400 members. They meet regionally on a regular basis to discuss strategic issues, hold lunchtime workshops to develop practical skills, hold periodic conferences and offer a useful sounding board and opportunity to network with other marketing people working in a similar environment.

A more recently formed body is The Marketing Council (TMC). This was set up in 1995 by leading British businessmen to promote the marketing concept within British industry at large, the perception being that too few companies in all sectors have embraced marketing properly. TMC's role is to act as a catalyst in encouraging organisations to self-help. Most of their efforts so far have been directed towards the consumer and industrial sectors, and it remains to be seen what they are able to generate within professional services.

All in all, marketing has come a long way in the last 13 years, as Edward Cleaveley predicted. Certainly the standard of marketing activities has risen appreciably. The employment of experienced practitioners has cut out much of the wastage and excessive charging that some external agencies were demanding and getting from surveyors who then did not know any better. Efficient use of the marketing function is looked at in Chapter 7. Most marketing activities – corporate and project – are in fact, now done rather well – certainly by the leading players.

What is only now beginning to happen is the impending revolution whereby firms become client-led to the extent that they are prepared to reshape themselves and tackle internal behavioural patterns in order to deliver to clients the services they seek, and profitably. This can only come if senior management embraces marketing in its full sense. What this means is covered in the next chapter.

Reference
1. **Cleaveley, E.** (1984)
The Marketing of Industrial and Commercial Property, LONDON: ESTATES GAZETTE.

Chapter 2

What is Marketing?

It is the nature of all marketing textbooks to define at the outset just what is meant by marketing. This rather suggests that most authors consider that the concept is still not properly understood.

We are all exposed to marketing activities every day of our lives, so it is hardly surprising that many business managers in the UK associate marketing with some of the more visible elements, such as advertising, media relations, mailing, that are carried out by marketing people. This is particularly the case within professional services in general and commercial property in particular, where marketing is a comparatively recent development. Most surveyors well understand some specific marketing activities, but too few have accepted the concept of marketing as an approach to running the business. In fact, marketing is a concept, as this chapter will endeavour to cover.

Defining marketing

A definition of marketing that would be acceptable to most marketing professionals is the established definition used by the Chartered Institute of Marketing (CIM): "Marketing is the management process responsible for identifying, anticipating and satisfying customer requirements profitably". This is fine as far as it goes, but since few non-marketing people understand what the "process" entails, then we need more than a definition, however acceptable. What is also required is a description of the process.

A simple illustration of marketing that may be useful is that "it is a radically different way of looking at running a business".

It is reasonable to accept that the traditional approach to business has been:

This approach works as long as the company can of course sell its product or service.

Unfortunately, various pressures combine to ensure that companies are most unlikely to be able to continue to sell their product or service for any length of time. The pressures may be short-term responses from competitors offering a similar product in a more attractive way or they may be the result of shifting consumer preferences over a longer period. Let us take, for example, the motor cycle. Annual sales of motor-cycles in the UK over the last 20 years show a market that has largely disappeared:

Fig 1	New motor-cycle sales in the UK 1975-95	
1975	1985	1995
284,767	125,996	54,140

Source: Motor Cycle Association, new registrations of mopeds, scooters, motor-cycles and three wheelers.

What has happened is that sales of machines as a means of cheap transport, particularly for young people, have substantially dried up. More and more people have switched to cars, often second-hand cars as these have become cheaper, more reliable and the population has become more affluent and safety conscious. The motorcycle units still sold are, for the most part, a core of sporting, higher performance bikes for enthusiasts. Some manufacturers failed to adapt to these changing customer needs and no longer exist. The future for those who remain probably depends on the sports or fashion appeal – an initiative which the industry was launching in late 1996.

There are numerous such examples both of whole sectors and individual companies coming to grief. Within our own commercial property sector there have been examples and in recent times at that. So how does marketing help to avoid failure? It does so by turning the whole approach to business on its head. Instead of the above, traditional approach, the marketing approach is:

This is a simplification of what the marketing concept is, but it is the core of marketing and all marketing practices stem from this standpoint.

Looking again at the CIM definition and comparing it with this marketing approach, with its implicit call for reorganisation and for an understanding of costs and margins, it can immediately be seen that marketing is the province of management. Indeed, if you accept that this marketing approach is a more likely route to successful corporate performance, then it is incumbent upon all would-be managers, and general management above all, to understand the concept and embrace it.

This is not to suggest that all managers need to become marketing people – any more than they need to become accountants, human resources or IT experts, but a good manager needs to understand the principles of marketing.

The role of the marketing department

If marketing is the remit of management, what then is the role of the marketing department? Indeed, is one needed? This is a question that has been raised in recent years within certain companies, typically in the fmcg (fast-moving consumer goods) area, where the marketing concept is very well understood by the majority of management and where marketing has become accepted as the driving force of the organisation.

In some cases the marketing department, as the main motor of marketing within the organisation, in consequence has become so powerful, so arrogant, that it has lost sight of the everyday realities of its market-place. To address this some companies have restructured to bring their marketing specialists within the fold of line operating units.

This situation, however, is not at all typical of the service sector. For the most part, marketing is still struggling to assert itself as an appropriate way of looking at business , rather than merely sales support or advertising. Positions of such power within the organisation have simply not been attained, let alone abused. One key role for the marketing department, therefore, is to try continually to encourage acceptance of the marketing concept by other managers.

In this, marketing people are unusual. Most professionals rarely try to explain their professional discipline. They even on occasions look to preserve a mystique about their work – be they doctors, lawyers, IT specialists or car mechanics. This no doubt helps protect their position and increases the fee levels they can charge.

Marketing professionals, on the other hand, are forever trying to explain their discipline. This is not to suggest that marketing people are more altruistic – there are practical reasons for this behaviour, related to gaining approval and resources to carry out marketing initiatives, but more of this later.

The other key role of the marketing department is to know how to execute the various specific practices that stem from the marketing concept. In this respect, they are like any other qualified professionals.

The marketing process

A marketing approach to business is simply a three-stage exercise:

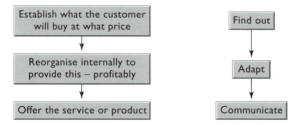

Each of these three broad stages covers a range of techniques and skills which will be looked at in more detail in subsequent chapters. Chapter 4, Finding out, will cover what it is that is worth finding out and the various ways of doing so; Chapter 5, Adapting, will look at what should be adapted and how it can be achieved; and Chapter 6, Communicating, will look at the various ways of communicating to the market and when each is appropriate. Some of the activities in each of the three stages are so complex and so developed that they are themselves the subjects of whole textbooks, with techniques so refined that individuals spend their working lives within that function. Examples of such jobs include:

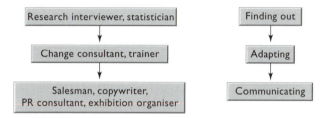

It is functions such as these possibly that will be more familiar to most people and which are more readily associated with marketing. What is less appreciated is that they are part of a co-ordinated, planned process aimed at achieving a pre-determined result. Within the process the Finding out and the Communicating elements particularly will be recognised. What is probably less familiar is the Adapt element, and yet that is the crux of marketing thinking: changing to meet market requirements. This pivotal role in the process requires the support of management in general, but within a marketing department it is classically the remit of the brand manager. This role tends not to exist within marketing departments in the property sector, but what this role entails for the marketing department and the organisation will be covered in Chapter 5.

It is probably worth dismantling here the notion that marketing is simply selling and advertising. These are, in fact, just two ways of telling the market about your products or services. They are therefore tools, albeit expensive ones, at the disposal of marketing, arrows in the quiver if you like – and they may or may not be appropriate within a marketing programme. Marketing is an altogether broader process of assessing a company's options and formulating programmes to help deliver performance.

There is one further point that needs to be made about this three-stage marketing process and it relates to Finding out. There are various ways of finding out what the market wants and in what way and at what price. One way, and it is often a good start point, is to analyse the existing business. This offers very hard information about clients' requirements and choices especially if tracked over time. It can provide a basic understanding for a company of "where it is now" and suggest what other areas of finding out need to be explored.

Existing performance is the direct result of client reaction to a supplier's activity in the market-place. It is also the reaction to competitors' activities and to changes in the market-place itself. This response tracking can, by definition, be held to be at the end of the marketing process:

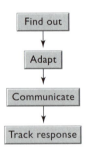

But response tracking is itself another means of finding out which brings us back to the beginning of the marketing process. The reality of course is that there is no beginning and no end. Markets are continuous and the interaction of buyers and suppliers of the services within them is constantly shifting. A more accurate description of the marketing process in practice therefore would be that it is circular and all the time moving forward:

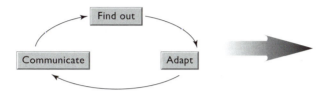

In this way each new marketing initiative will be the result of having established what clients want, and having reorganised to be able to deliver it profitably. It will then be launched to the market, and the market reaction will be monitored for further adjustment. Hopefully this will be fine-tuning only if the initial market readings were sound. Over time, however, competitors will react with their own initiatives and client expectations will inevitably shift, prompting more fundamental adjustment.

As we saw in the example of the motor-cycle industry, client expectations can sometimes shift to the extent that an entire product or service sector is threatened. This often comes when suppliers of products or services fail to maintain their understanding of why customers are buying. Companies concentrate too closely on their existing role and fail to see a threat coming from an often different quarter, which may undermine their whole sector. This failing was described as long ago as 1960 as "marketing myopia" by Theodore Levitt, Professor at Harvard Business School.[1]

Levitt said: "The railroads did not stop growing because the need for passenger and freight transportation declined. That grew. The railroads are in trouble today *not* because the need was filled by others (cars, trucks, aeroplanes, even telephones) but because it was not filled by the railroads themselves. They let others take customers away from them because they assumed themselves to be in the railroad business rather than in the transportation business. The reason they defined their industry wrong was because they were railroad-oriented instead of transportation-oriented; they were product-oriented instead of customer-oriented."

Levitt offers little sympathy for those companies who do not track what it is their clients seek, and precisely what client needs they are satisfying: "In every case the reason growth is threatened, slowed or stopped is *not* because the market is saturated. It is because there has been a failure of management."

With the excess of stock developed in the late 1980s and the amount of downsizing considered necessary in the property industry in the 1990s it is legitimate to ask how much research into client needs and expectations has been carried out. Clearly there is no resting on laurels and the marketing function in any organisation should be actively pressing to establish market needs and to change and improve the organisation's response.

Service marketing and product marketing

So far the concept of marketing has been examined without distinguishing between marketing a service and marketing a product. In the world of commercial property both needs exist: those players within the market, be they investors, developers, occupiers, consultants, agents or whatever, all need to market themselves and the services they offer; at the same time most of these players will be involved in the marketing of the tangible products that are land and buildings.

I have deliberately not drawn a distinction between the concept of product marketing and the concept of service marketing. That is because the concept, the approach, the thought processes should all be consistent. This applies even to fmcg and professional services. The thought processes for marketing baked beans need be no different from marketing, say, a firm of surveyors. What is very different, however, is the practice and application of marketing.

Too often, professional firms have hired sophisticated fmcg marketing staff only for them to fail, with resultant disappointment on both sides. My observation is that this has most often been the product of attempts to apply fmcg *practices* directly in the service area. Often the basic tenet of marketing: know your customer, has been ignored. Services are much more complex to market than products, as we shall explore in Chapter

5. The further main failing has been an inability to effect sufficient change within the professional service supplier – the culture is too resistant. Sadly this means not only the failure of the marketing initiative, but if it continues to happen – as Levitt suggests – it will lower the performance of the company.

In the same way that the approach is constant but the practice varies between product and service marketing, so, within the property industry, the practice of marketing a property varies from the practice of marketing a company or service. We shall look at the marketing of property in Section II of this book, even considering whether it can properly be termed marketing. In Section I, which follows, we shall concentrate on Corporate or service marketing.

Reference:

REPRINTED BY PERMISSION OF HARVARD BUSINESS REVIEW. EXCERPT FROM THEODORE LEVITT, *Marketing Myopia*, HARVARD BUSINESS REVIEW. (SEPTEMBER-OCTOBER 1975)

Section **One**

Marketing companies and services

Chapter 3

Can marketing be applied to a professional service?

There are still, regrettably, some who subscribe to the view that marketing is not appropriate within a professional service environment. I first came across this notion in the 1970s, when I was Marketing Manager at what was then Williams & Glyn's Bank (now The Royal Bank of Scotland). I well remember visiting our Derby branch. This was one of the most successful branches in the country: a large, growing client base and highly profitable. I wanted to find out why. I was met at Derby station by the branch manager and within minutes I knew why.

On the brief trip from station to branch, the manager said to me: "You'd better know now Martin, I've no time for this marketing. I believe in finding out what my customers want and giving it to them at a profit to the Bank." This is pretty close to the Find Out, Adapt, Communicate – at a profit – process set out in Chapter 2 as being what marketing is. With such fundamental common ground it is hardly surprising that we got on fine the rest of the day, though I am not sure he liked being called a good marketing man.

Most good professionals would subscribe to the Derby banker's view of sensible business management. It is difficult to see where the notion comes from that marketing is not appropriate and why there is an aversion to it. It can only be due to a lack of understanding, or a misunderstanding, of what marketing is. The popular view of marketing, as already suggested, is that it is about advertising, selling, brochures, PR – all elements of the communicating bit of marketing. This is hardly surprising since these are the very visible aspects of marketing. The finding out and adapting processes of marketing are largely unseen and consequently less well understood.

A marketing professional, on the other hand, sees the visible promotion activities within the context of an overall business development aim, and judges each according to its ability to meet the particular need. Because non-marketing people are not versed in the uses and value of activities, such as advertising or mailing within their overall context, they judge them in isolation and subjectively.

A lack of understanding of marketing is a serious charge. Lest I be accused of unfairly making this charge, examples of this might be: setting the marketing budget without reference to the business plan; reducing marketing staff and budgets "because we cannot afford them"; not carrying out regular market research; launching service lines without research; and so on. Most readers can probably identify a competitor who doesn't understand marketing.

There may be a legacy within some professional services from the days, not so many years ago, when overt competition between firms was frowned upon and indeed discouraged and restricted by the professional governing bodies. It is my impression though that these days are in the cosy past as far as the property sector is concerned.

There is also a discomfort factor in the marketing of services. It has been said often enough that many have been attracted to the professions because they did not wish to be involved in selling or self-promotional activities. I think there is some truth in this, though it probably applies less to commercial property than to other professions.

In fact, within a service industry in particular, there are elements that generate discomfort at all stages of the marketing process:

Finding out   –   research costs money
             –   it means others having access to my clients
             –   criticism might get personal

Adapting   –   personal reluctance to change working practices
             –   training costs time and money

Telling   –   costs money
             –   much of the spend is wasted
             –   subjective dislike of advertising, mailing, brochures, selling, etc.

The reality is, for most of us anyway, that we no longer live in a comfortable, non-competitive world. The notion that marketing is in some way not appropriate within professional services was probably never valid. Good professionals – like the Derby bank manager - will have adopted a marketing approach without recognising or calling it such.

In subsequent chapters the various marketing activities will be looked at in more detail and the individual appropriateness of each explored. The concept, however, of meeting customers needs profitably, as outlined in the previous chapter, simply has to be appropriate to a professional service. Indeed, I would go so far as to say any professional service company not embracing marketing is being unprofessional.

Where marketing a service is different

This does not mean that all marketing practices are relevant to the property sector. Where marketing does vary by industry is in its application. Within the commercial property sector, there is a difference between the marketing of a company and its services, and the marketing of property. Property is tangible and more akin to a product, and this marketing will be looked at further in Section II of this book. Section I considers the application of marketing to an organisation within the service environment, or corporate marketing.

The basic conceptual approach already outlined will work both for a consumer product and for a professional service, and the same marketing thought processes need to be applied. Where service marketing and product marketing differ is in the **application** of Finding out, Adapting and Communicating.

The essential difference between product and service marketing revolves around what the customer is buying. With a product, be it a consumer or a business product, the item being bought will have certain properties and functions that are determinable. The proverbial can of beans will have a mix of defined contents and come in a prescribed format.

The contents will even be listed, as required by law, in volume order on the can label, e.g.

Ingredients:		
	Beans	*Salt*
	Water	*Modified cornflour*
	Tomatoes	*Spirit vinegar*
	Sugar	*Spices*

The range of issues the customer considers when buying will be apparent to the customer and, if the bean company has done its research, will be known to the supplier. The supplier will have adjusted the can of beans to meet customer needs. The adjustment may have been one of contents, it may have been in the packaging, the price, or the point of sale. All, however, will be definable and physically adjustable, albeit at a price.

Service marketing is much tougher for these very reasons. What satisfies the customer is less easily defined and is less easily adjusted. Chapter 5 will look in more detail at what it is the customer buys and what therefore might need to be adjusted, but it is immediately obvious that the key difference from buying a product is the human interaction entailed in buying a service. By definition a service is performed by a person or several people. The service may well entail a core product element or a core professional skill, for example the property audit or leasing, but it would be most unusual for a service buyer to make the purchase decision solely on the strength of this and not to be influenced in some way by the way people deliver the service.

Over time, if the customer is repeatedly buying the service then there is every possibility that the interaction will move on from being a series of buying decisions and develop into a relationship. The loyalty and trust this implies make it attractive for the service supplier to develop relationships. At this stage what the purchaser is buying has shifted, embracing a more complex series of satisfactions way over and above the basic professional skill.

It follows that marketing needs to identify and adjust any factors that might positively affect the client's propensity to buy and to help to build the relationship. The factors may well differ between clients, for example US or Asian corporates may have different expectations from their European counterparts. Private individuals may act quite differently again. The factors may be broad ranging, taking in various aspects of staff performance. The client may not even readily identify each aspect even though it is real.

To illustrate the complexity of a service product, take the example of a restaurant. Imagine that the need you wish to satisfy is to enjoy a pleasant evening, dining out with someone who is close to you. Within a reasonable journey time from your home there are many restaurants potentially competing for your custom. In choosing which one to go to, you might take into account many factors.

As with any service offer, at the heart of the service is the core skill, the professionalism on which the offer is based. In the case of a restaurant we can assume that the core skill is the ability of the chef in the kitchen. It may well be that, for you, this is the dominant consideration in deciding where to dine, but it is unlikely to be the only factor – and, if you are lucky, there may be three or four equally good chefs within striking distance. To differentiate between them you may well consider some of the factors listed below:

Fig 2	The service product – a restaurant

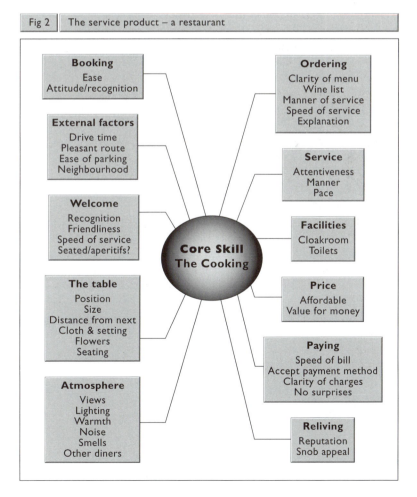

Some of these considerations may be unimportant when making your choice; some may only become important if they are done badly. For each of us the weight we give each factor will be different. Even your own dining companion will attach a different significance to each factor.

The human element

What is immediately apparent from the list, which I do not pretend is exhaustive, is that most of the factors are dependent upon the people delivering them. At the core is the chef in the kitchen producing what arrives on your plate. But even here there may be other people involved – and the grander the restaurant the more likely this is. The buying of the ingredients, the preparation of the food for cooking, the cooking itself may all have involved a team of people under the chef's command.

Outside the kitchen there may be the receptionist who answers the telephone to take the booking, the host who greets you, waiter(s) and wine waiter. Each of the team involved has the opportunity to help your evening be more enjoyable or to spoil it. And what might please one guest could be unwelcome to another. A restaurateur needs to recognise all these issues and seek to control them in order to deliver a successful service. Much of his or her energy will be spent on recruiting, training and retaining the right calibre of staff, but, in doing so, he or she must have in mind the level and nature of service required in order to satisfy clients profitably.

Chapter 5 will look at the nature of the service provided in commercial property and what aspects of the service the supplier should seek to control. The restaurant example demonstrates that the range of client motivations can be both complex and varied. The contents of the service cannot, like the can of beans, be listed in volume order.

This is what makes the marketing process of Finding out more difficult for a service than a product. The need to find out, however, is every bit as great. The restaurant owner must establish where there is a sufficient body of potential clients; what the transport/parking facilities are in each location option; and what importance diners place on the various internal considerations, so that the more significant ones and potentially damaging ones can be tackled first. The need then is to adapt the overall service offer to the identified demand.

It should not be assumed that the core skill is necessarily the most important factor. There are many restaurants that survive successfully by providing what experts would rate as merely satisfactory food, but in an attractive atmosphere. Different buyers look for different experiences. It is likely, however, that in business-to-business services the core skill will rate highly and may even be the *sine qua non*.

Even corporate buyers, however, may have a limited ability to judge the core professional skill. Few of us can be sure that we have received the best legal advice or the best property valuation. Certainly I have seen many examples in commercial property of companies buying bad marketing help from external service providers.

Service buying is tougher to define than product buying because the service variables are that much greater. Similarly, the process of adapting the service is that much more complex. The key distinction is that the service the client is buying is, in part at least, the person or persons delivering it. In some services the personality or style of the person delivering the service may be so strong as to dominate all other considerations: artists, musicians and libel lawyers are good examples of this. Even major organisations can owe much of their appeal to the personality of one or two of the organisations' personnel, e.g. Virgin and Richard Branson, The Body Shop and Anita Roddick.

Given the potential importance of personality, and the inevitable human element entailed, adapting the service poses a challenge With a product it is relatively easy to design each version of the product to be the same – indeed that is the promise. Buy a Mars bar and you know exactly what you will get, every time. Failure to get the promised ingredients in a product, or getting an unexpected ingredient could lead to legal redress.

What is the promise?

So, what is the promise from a service supplier with maybe a hundred or more staff all helping to deliver the service? With some service lines it is possible to design the process of delivery in such a developed and detailed way that the service acquires almost the uniformity of a consumer product.

McDonald's have very successfully achieved this by concentrating on every aspect of the total service and working hard to instil performance standards wherever the service is offered. On the property front, for example, they have now, through prefabrication of standard units, reduced the time required from breaking the ground to serving the first customer to as little as two weeks in some instances. Their recruitment policies, training and staff incentive programmes are similarly geared to ensuring that the McDonald's service promise is delivered consistently in terms both of standards and friendly, enthusiastic style. But fast food companies recruit younger, more malleable staff and put them in uniforms. The prospect of a professional services firm demanding a similarly cloned performance, both in process and in style, from its partners and staff is limited.

The reality is that the culture of most professional service firms is too resistant: resistant to suppression of individual character traits; resistant even to change itself. This is even more manifest in a partnership. A strong argument against personal uniformity is that clients differ and building relationships with a range of clients requires a range of in-house personalities. This is in fact recognising the very human element of service provision and allowing for a mix of personalities to attract a mix of clients. This makes sound marketing sense. Where adapting should then be effected is in defining the standards of performance required and range of expertise to be delivered by each individual.

As with Adapting, the process of delivery to the client is again different for a service for the very same reason, the human element. The aspects that can be defined and controlled are the standards required and the following through of concerted business development initiatives. The issue of sales force control will be discussed in Chapter 6, but it is inevitable that an organisation that directs, supports and rewards its sales staff for seeking targeted business in a co-ordinated way is going to be more successful.

Historically such co-ordination has not been the norm in commercial property, nor in many other professions, but the signs are that some firms are now doing something about this and generating controlled business development programmes. A necessary precursor to this is securing agreement to the targets and the programmes to be adopted. Typically this agreement is secured through the firm's business planning. The link between business planning and marketing will be covered in Chapter 7.

The next chapter looks at the Finding out process, examining what market studies are sensible and what use should be made of them. There should, however, be little doubt that marketing is not only entirely appropriate within professional services, but that organisations who ignore it or do it badly are on borrowed time.

Chapter 4

Marketing in practice: Finding out

I had worked in the property sector a matter of weeks when somebody put to me that marketing was about helping you to get from A to B. I agreed, but added that it was first about finding out where A was, what the options were and whether B was the most attractive, and only then determining how to get there. This somewhat coded discussion pointed up the flawed perception that marketing services are all marketing is, and the lack of appreciation that effective marketing starts with research.

On one level the research undertaken within the sector is prodigious. The quality and volume of studies on the commodity that is commercial property is highly impressive. Increasingly too, sophisticated clients are employing the research departments of leading surveying firms to undertake viability studies for them before locating.

Given the recognition, even the promotion, of the idea that gathering information is a necessary risk-reducing step before taking action, it is surprising that so little formal research into client needs has been conducted in the sector. Chapter 2 emphasised the fundamental need to establish what the client wants if a firm genuinely seeks to satisfy those needs profitably. Dr. Neil Morgan, Lecturer in Marketing & Strategy at Cambridge University, said in his excellent *Professional Services Marketing book* (1991) that "a firm cannot begin to really become a client-centred, market-oriented business without undertaking some form of marketing research to identify specifically, and in detail, exactly what clients needs are..." [1]. And yet it remains the case that not just in commercial property but across professional services in general, too little client research is conducted.

Resistance to research

Before moving on to examine what should be found out and the various ways of going about it, what is it that is inhibiting more research activity? Discussion with other marketing professionals suggests that they would like to do more research but enthusiasm is limited among management. They tell me a number of counter-arguments have typically been put by management:

"Research only tells us what we already know"

Even if this were the case, there would be value in having external, objective confirmation of views held. It reduces uncertainty and allows the whole firm to respond more confidently. This clearly is worth something. In practice, however, "what **we** already know" varies depending on which individual is talking. It is my long experience that client handlers, across various business sectors, have gaps in their knowledge, particularly when it comes to broader business issues.

"You can't trust the findings"

Usually it is sampling, methodology or interviewer incompetence that are mentioned. This argument sits uncomfortably with the first objection, and together they provide management with the opportunity to have their own views only supported and never challenged. This suggests a frightening level of self-complacency and yet, recalling the Chartered Surveyors Survey (published annually until 1995) it was the norm for firms to criticise the study and demolish unwelcome findings, whilst at the same time basking in the glory of welcome high ratings.

Of course, some research agencies are not good, some interviewers poor, some sampling/methodology inappropriate for the task. Interpretation of findings too can be variable. The Chartered Surveyors Survey, for instance, was somewhat quirky in its interpretation of rankings and, depending on the scoring system adopted, widely differing results could be obtained. But this is addressed through proper briefing, agency selection and interpretation – all covered later in this chapter. The fact remains that management cannot have it both ways. Research findings have to be taken with an open mind. Ignoring them or not seeking them in the first place is to run risks in the management of the organisation.

"You can interpret the findings any way you want"

If the project has been briefed and structured properly, the possibility of varied interpretation will be minimised. Questionnaire design is a highly developed skill and professional help is needed here. While at times there is room for interpretation (hopefully balanced), if precise findings are needed the research can be so structured to provide them.

"I can ask clients myself"

This of course is true though, for a number of reasons, it is a bad idea. Questions are less likely to be asked objectively and more likely to be coloured; feedback similarly; the clients selected are unlikely to be the more vociferously critical ones and, therefore, may be unrepresentative; and many clients are more likely to "pull their punches" if being interviewed by the service provider. Further, clients are by definition a specific group within the market as a whole and non-clients, potential clients, lapsed clients may all have a very different set of views (see Healey & Baker case study, below).

"It's not worth the money"

This is the hardest argument to refute. So much marketing expenditure is an investment where the cost can readily be seen, but the return is less easily quantified, however justifiable professionally it might seem. Where the topic being researched is specific then some attempt can be made at valuing the findings. A confirmation to proceed brings comfort; a warning not to go ahead can save financial loss. The research is akin to an insurance policy. Where the study is more broadly based then the investment is an act of faith – that enough will come out of the study to help reshape and improve the firm's competitive effectiveness.

The purpose of research

Improving competitive effectiveness should be what drives the entire research programme. Whether the research takes the form of internal information gathering or a formal, external market study, it is important to identify at the outset:

1. What are we trying to find out?

2. What will we do with the findings?

As long as the information gathering process is seen as the first stage in reshaping and meeting clients needs, then the answers to these two questions should be known. Where the research programme can occasionally come adrift from the rest of the marketing effort is when there is a separate market research department with its own manager and, worse, its own budget. This tends to happen in larger service organisations and I am not aware of any such situations within commercial property. I would recommend strongly that market research is an integral part of the marketing department. In this way, those charged with reshaping and communicating are those who determine what information needs to be gathered.

The second point, using the findings, may seem to be so obvious as to not need stating. There is a danger, and again it is more likely to occur when the research function becomes detached, of research for research sake, whereby information is gathered that may be "interesting" but incapable of being used to achieve anything.

By way of example, corporate image research can go off the rails, partly because the task is a sensitive one. Wrapped in with the image of any firm will be the personalities of individual partners or directors. This complicates the exercise in a number of ways:

- Lack of enthusiasm among decision makers for fear of attracting possible personal criticism
- Reluctance to accept findings if they are unwelcome
- Variability of individual and corporate images
- Subjectivity of response, depending on individual contact
- Limited likelihood of effecting significant personality change

Research companies have various ways of tackling this sensitive task and some, in their efforts to de-personalise the issue, come up with bizarre concepts. One I have heard of asked clients "If firm X were a car, what model would it be?". Whilst there are broad assumptions to be drawn if one is characterised as a Lada rather than a Rolls-Royce, the failings of this sort of approach are: that different interviewees will have widely varying knowledge of, and image of, car models so one man's BMW might be another man's Alfa Romeo; and ultimately so what? The information is not readily usable.

For all this, corporate image is critical and needs to be addressed. (The importance of branding will be covered in Chapter 6.) Most leading firms have in fact done so in recent years, as evidenced by two case studies, below and in Chapter 6.

Where to start

At the beginning of the chapter, I suggested that marketing started with understanding the organisation's present position. By this I mean both current trading performance and position within the market. There are various sources of information on both and, whether they are formal research exercises or in-house data, they can all contribute to the first Finding out stage of marketing. The following lists some of the intelligence gathering processes that are available.

Internal sources   —   sales figures
  —   sales force feedback
  —   repeat business

Published sources   —   government figures
  —   Trade Association reports
  —   industry studies
  —   media comment

Client feedback   —   letters
  —   comments at conferences/exhibitions

Research studies   —   commissioned work, carried out internally or through external agencies

It follows that the start point in determining the organisation's present position is to analyse the information base, the sales figures, that already exists in-house. Quite apart from the benefit of knowing where you're starting from, this intelligence should prove to be the quickest to gather and the cheapest. Obviously if the data within the organisation is to be collated and summarised to produce meaningful management information, it follows that those who wish to analyse the data - and this includes the marketing team - must play their part in designing the intelligence database to deliver data in a usable form.

Published sources and media comment should be tapped for market performance because they too are comparatively cheap and quick to absorb. The combined intelligence gathered will paint a picture of current performance. It should show what business is being conducted and with whom, and suggest how strong a position within the market the firm holds, by client type and by service line.

Stemming from this will be a number of strategic judgements. A firm where 10% of clients are producing 90% of fees has a whole different set of strengths and potential problems from the firm where 10% are producing 50%. The implications for account handling, pricing, cross-selling, investment in business development and promotion are immediately apparent.

Analysis such as this will also inevitably help an organisation to understand where its profits come from. What the marketing function needs to know is, not so much which internal units are delivering the profits, as much as which client types and service lines. It may be that the internal costing regime is not so highly developed (and developing it brings its own significant costs) as to allow for precise profitability assessment by client or service, but broad assumptions can and should be made. Translating these findings into marketing action will be covered in more detail in Chapter 7, but first and foremost they will enable an organisation to determine who should be its targets.

Targeting

Defining target clients or sectors is of such fundamental importance that I imagine most readers would confidently recognise their own organisation's stated targets. Targeting can, however, be inadequate in a number of respects:

Selecting target groups

All too often organisations group and analyse clients according to their own business operations. An example I recall from my financial service days is that of "mid-range corporates". Banks analysed their corporate client work according to the trading size of the company. They then extended the "mid range corporates" tag through internal restructuring and even to promoting.

In doing this they missed two points: a target group should be able to readily identify itself as the target, and I am not sure how many CEOs go round thinking "I'm a mid-range corporate"; and, secondly, a target group must be readily approachable as that group, and I cannot think of any media such as "Mid-range Corporates Monthly". This left the banks with a lengthy and very expensive promotional task, with considerable media wastage. It may be necessary, for the collation of the relevant expertise, for an internal function to concentrate on mid-range corporates, business space or whatever, but promoting this to the market is flawed.

Starting, even before analysis, by splitting targets into how they identify themselves and are approachable will concentrate thinking on clients' needs. This has implications for database design which need to be addressed.

Defining non-targets

It is as important to determine what business is not attractive as it is to identify targets. It may be unattractive for a variety of reasons: limited market size, unstable companies, risky sector, margins too fine, lack of specialist knowledge, competition too severe, etc. Whatever the reason or reasons the organisation should feel comfortable about accepting that there is certain business it will not go for.

Internal communication

It is vital that staff know who are the targets and who are not. Every selling organisation has this problem to some degree. Employing commission only agents and rewarding them only for gaining specified business is perhaps the surest way of controlling targeting. This, though, brings with it other issues, some of which are weaknesses, such as ensuring common service standards and cultural fit. In an organisation that allows its staff, including directors or partners, a degree of choice in how they spend their time, it is imperative that they all have a clear understanding of the organisation's targets. The communication of this should be two-way. They should input to the agreement of targets. Each organisation will have its own range of internal communication processes, starting with the business plan. This is dealt with in chapter 7. The dialogue generated will add significantly to the level of market intelligence held within the organisation.

So far, with the exception of field force feedback, the sources discussed have been those that provide quantitative data only. This is necessary for understanding where the organisation is and where it might want to go. It does not, however, explain why current performance is what it is nor does it suggest how the goals might be achieved. Qualitative information is required to do this. From the list above, the following sources can offer this:

- sales force feedback
- industry studies
- media comment
- client feedback
- research studies

By definition, each source is looking at issues from a different standpoint and this may colour the information accordingly. The answer is to utilise all these sources to build a better understanding of why clients behave as they do and why your firm performs as it does.

As already suggested, too little use is made of the last source – formal research studies. The other sources, however, are all vigorously digested. They all have the merit of costing very little and should be utilised first before developing any formal study. Formal research is relatively expensive, certainly compared with all the other forms of intelligence gathering. It follows, therefore, that the more precise the brief and the more defined the areas of study, then the more effective the expenditure is likely to be. Defining the brief and the scope of the study will be facilitated if the other sources have been tapped first and some understanding of the market already obtained.

Why formal research is vital

Any organisation wishing to understand its market and itself needs to undertake formal market research. The other sources on their own, even collectively, are simply not enough. Industry studies and media comment will rarely offer in-depth coverage of one organisation; sales force and client feedback will be entirely pertinent to the organisation but they are, by definition, a limited sample, and possibly an unrepresentative sample. These sources will filter views selectively and of course will apply to existing rather than potential clients. Formal research on the other hand will cover adequate samples of the target groups, be they existing or potential clients and, in being carried out by a third party, is much more likely to provide objective, balanced and honest responses. Organisations are frankly deluding themselves if they think they do not need to carry out external studies.

What the composite qualitative picture will give is a sharper guide to what it is clients are looking for, how they want it delivered, how they determine between one supplier and another, and how strongly or weakly the service supplier is perceived. This intelligence is critical in pointing the way to change and improvement.

Once the shape and form of clients' requirements is known, the assessment needs to be made as to whether the demand has sufficient profit potential to justify corporate reaction. The research now needs to shift to quantitative study.

The methodology, sampling and questionnaire design are all quite different from the qualitative stage. Research is at its most potent when different types of research are used in concert – each contributing to the build-up of intelligence and understanding of the market.

Figure 3 sets out a typical process of intelligence gathering:

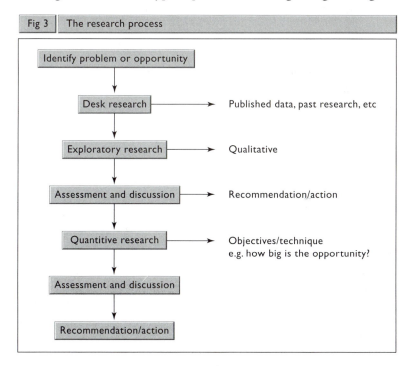

Fig 3	The research process

Identify problem or opportunity

Desk research → Published data, past research, etc

Exploratory research → Qualitative

Assessment and discussion → Recommendation/action

Quantitive research → Objectives/technique
e.g. how big is the opportunity?

Assessment and discussion

Recommendation/action

Given the increasingly international nature of the commercial property market, it follows that the process of understanding the market, the client and the organisation itself takes on an increased complexity. Even within Europe, there remain substantial operating differences between individual country markets; varying levels of client expectation; and varying capabilities and performance of the service providers. If business performance is to be managed at all, these differences and variations need to be understood.

With most professional activities it is very easy to perform badly if you are not properly qualified. The same applies to research, where there is capacity to slip up at every stage: sampling, methodology, interviewing, questionnaire design, interpretation. Given that the whole purpose of research is to help insure against mistakes and/or provide the pointers for reshaping corporate performance, it makes sense to employ people who know what they are doing and to devote sufficient time to explaining to them what you are looking for. Happily, in the UK we are blessed with many, excellent research organisations, arguably more so than anywhere else in the world.

Selecting an agency

In selecting an agency, if you or your colleagues do not know of a good agency there are many sources of guidance: the Market Research Society, the Industrial Marketing Research Association, the Chartered Institute of Marketing, The Marketing Society, and the Professional Services Marketing Group can all offer help. Good advice would be to use a specialist research firm and to beware of using a general advertising, PR or marketing agency. Ensure too that the research company is recognised by a professional body and bound by its Code of Conduct. Research is a specialist activity and other, or general, marketing agencies are unlikely to have sufficient skills.

Selecting a research firm will not be a difficult task, provided that you know what information you are seeking and explain this fully to the research company. Research consultant Karen Randolph offers the following list of Do's and Don'ts:

1. Brief the consultant or agency thoroughly. Give them the background and the context. Don't imagine the agency, even

if they have done similar work for you before, knows what you know about the product or the market – or your problem. Researchers much prefer to be given too much information than too little. If part of a syndicate commissioning research, it is particularly important to take the initiative if you want to get maximum benefit from the project.

2. Decide which company has best shown an appreciation of the problem.

3. Be open minded about alternative solutions suggested by the research company.

4. Consider the experience and expertise of the companies, but precise experience of narrow sectors should not be regarded as a prerequisite – a good market researcher should be able to pick up the essential details quickly.

5. Decide which company has convinced you that their proposed research method or combination of methods best suits the job. Often all methods suggested can do the job but which sounds the best to you?

6. Make sure that you and your staff feel that you can work with the agency chosen and the individuals in that agency – a good rapport is very important. Many a project has suffered because of personality clashes.

7. Don't worry about expressing ignorance about market research techniques – professional researchers much prefer to be asked to discuss fully any aspects of research, for example the pros and cons of qualitative research versus quantitative research.

8. If possible visit the agencies concerned, or the agency selected, to see their facilities – in particular the field force – and familiarise yourself with the processes involved.

9. When agreeing the timing, keep in touch with the agency at specific stages, e.g. at the start of field work, when raw data is received, etc. If some delay is met, check how this will affect the completion date.

10. Don't select only on basis of cost and/or time.

Research methodology

The research techniques selected will be driven by what information is sought. Exploratory research into why markets exist, what new services might be launched or what promotional messages will work, will require qualitative techniques.

In many sectors, particularly consumer sectors, group discussions may be used. These usually consist of a specially recruited group of 6-10 people led and guided by a trained moderator. These are useful in exploring new concepts or sensitive issues in that they are less intimidating than an individual in-depth interview. The discussion will be likely to be more creative and broad ranging, and social and cultural differences within the group will come out.

Possible problems that can arise are dominance by one or two strong characters, and some members may be more reluctant to discuss sensitive issues. Much also depends on the skill and experience of the moderator. Where corporate service buyers are concerned, it is not easy to recruit a group of senior people to be available at a given time, or to give the length of time (typically a couple of hours) required. They are consequently expensive and, to my knowledge, have been used very little within the commercial property sector. Their best uses are for concept testing, such as a new service, or for image testing.

The other principal technique of qualitative research and the one most used in the sector, is the in-depth personal interview. The advantages are obvious: personal opinions can be explored in depth, decision-making processes can be analysed, strength of feeling and range of feelings stressed, discussion points can be developed. The disadvantages are that it is a time- consuming and costly process.

With both group discussions and individual interviews it is important that the moderator or interviewer is experienced enough to win the respect of the interviewee and sensitive enough to recognise when to explore further different issues arising in the session. In either case it is usually possible to ascertain the range of issues from speaking with a small number of people.

Measuring the frequency with which views are held, or how many clients behave in a certain way - quantitative research - requires larger numbers to be interviewed. How much larger is discussed under sampling below. Interviews can be carried out face to face, at home, at work or in the street; by telephone or by mail.

Face-to-face interviews give a greater control over who is responding and lessen the likelihood of misunderstanding. Sensitive issues can be explored better and, obviously, reaction to visual material gauged. As with qualitative work, good interviewers are required and the cost is correspondingly high.

Telephone interviews have the advantage, to both commissioning client and the respondent, of being quickly completed. The location of the respondent is relatively unimportant, unless the study is international. This is very relevant in business-to-business research as it is frequently necessary to call several times to find a convenient time for the respondent and this becomes costly. The biggest constraint is that the interviewer cannot see the respondent's reaction to questions or show visual material.

Postal questionnaires have the advantages of being cheap and without possible interviewer bias. The weaknesses are that response rates can be low (though business-to-business generates good returns); response can be slow; those responding may not be typical; and there is less control over who does respond. Given that there is no interaction at all between an interviewer and the respondent, a greater onus is placed on the design of the questionnaire.

Questionnaire design is one of the most important stages of a research exercise. Any questionnaire needs to be ordered logically to encourage the respondent, and the information required must be clear and unambiguous. Some questions will be better given a simple choice of pre-determined responses, others will have to be open-ended in allowing the interviewee to express views more freely. The way questions are phrased is vital. It is very easy to fall into such traps as leading the respondent, e.g.

"Q. Do you feel goods are likely to be fresher in a supermarket due to higher turnover?"

or of trying to cover too many points, e.g.

"Q. At your local grocers, do you buy meat, fruit and cereals?"

The ordering and phrasing of each question is again a job for an expert who will design the questionnaire to reflect the overall aims of the study.

With any formal research study the aim is to have sufficient confidence in the results to take corporate decisions. The level of confidence that can safely be placed depends in part on the sample size. Sampling is by definition an estimate only of how a total body of people reacts. Patently the larger the sample size the more confidence can be placed in the results. There are formulae by which researchers can calculate the sample size required to deliver 90%, 95%, 99.7% levels and so on. The aim always will be to contain the sample to limit costs, while at the same time preserving sufficient confidence in the information gathered.

What constitutes the right level will partly depend on the issues covered, and on the degree to which responses are to be analysed by type of respondent. The more sub-groups of respondent to be analysed, the greater the sample required. This need will be exaggerated when it is minority sub-groups whose views are required. In such cases it will be better to construct a weighted sample, drawn from those sub-groups, rather than a much larger sample selected at random.

Interpretation

The issue of confidence needs to be reflected in the interpretation of research findings. There is a natural desire to see distinct views emerging from research and a tendency to present responses as truths. This is demonstrated in the fashionable obsession with percentages and decimal points which often suggest a level of accuracy which the methodology and sample size simply cannot support. It is nonsense, for example, to use decimal points where the sample size is less than 100, and misleading where the sample is less than say 300.

All of the caveats we have looked at in relation to methodology, sampling, interviewer skills, questionnaire design can be applied again to interpretation. Objectivity and honesty are called for in analysing and interpreting findings. For example a typical response from a sample to a question might be:

In favour	20%
Neither for nor against	40%
Against	20%
Don't know	20%

The protagonist might say "only 20% are against" while the antagonist could counter "only 20% are in favour". The figure that matters will depend on what is being measured and the use to be made of the data. An assessment of potential market size might be 80%, of likely short-term market size 20%, while the high incidence of Don't Knows and Undecideds (60%) suggests more education/information is necessary. The safest way to ensure an objective assessment of the research findings is carried out, with an understanding of the limitations, is to have it done by a professional researcher.

There is, I fear, a risk in highlighting some of the pitfalls and limitations of formal research that the reader may feel that it is all too complex and suspect to support. This would be a grave mistake. Research is a complex activity like any other professional exercise. Inadequately prepared and executed property work would produce similarly unsatisfactory results, but there will be few readers I suspect who would advocate dispensing with it. Research can be carried out with confidence provided that the person commissioning it knows what he or she wishes to find out; knows what use will be made of the findings; and uses professional help.

The next chapter looks at making use of all the intelligence gathering to adapt what it is the organisation offers to meet its client's identified needs.

Reference
1. Morgan, N.A. (1991)
Professional Services Marketing, LONDON: BUTTERWORTH-HEINEMANN.

Case study 1: Client research

Background

In 1989 Healey & Baker decided it needed a better appreciation of how the firm was perceived. A comparatively new management team had analysed the market and was taking a number of far-reaching strategic decisions: international expansion; not to open regional offices within the UK; investment in IT; recruitment of senior management in specialist functions, etc. At this important juncture, they wished to take stock of perceptions in the market. The firm recognised the value of appointing an independent research agency to carry out the study and commissioned IFT Marketing Research (now Gordon Simmons Research).

The brief

Healey & Baker wanted to know not only what its own clients thought, but also the general market view. The firm also wished to understand the market's perception of its strengths and weaknesses by comparison with leading competitors.

The agreed objectives of the study were:

1.   To measure awareness and image of H&B;
2.   To assess perceived strengths and weaknesses of H&B;
3.   To explore specific aspects of the services provided by H&B;
4.   To provide feedback of use to H&B in agreeing upon future corporate identity.

Methodology

The remit for the study was a broad one. It needed to cover a range of issues and speak to a broad cross-section of clients and non-clients. To meet these needs the study was carried out in two stages. Stage 1 consisted of 37 face-to-face interviews conducted by senior interviewers. The sample consisted of 18 H&B clients and 19 non-clients, split regionally and by broad business sector.

The questionnaire consisted largely of open-ended questions to give the respondents the opportunity to express their attitudes and opinions freely.

e.g. *"What would you say are the most important characteristics you would seek in a commercial property firm?"*

"What image do you have of each of the following commercial property firms?"

"Have you had any contact with Healey & Baker in the last year?"

"How impressive were they in comparison with contact from other firms?"

The information provided by the in-depth interviews was of a diagnostic nature – identifying perceptions and attitudes but not necessarily confirming them. Further research at Stage 2 was undertaken in order to satisfy this requirement.

Stage 2 consisted of a further 100 telephone interviews (41 clients and 59 non-clients). The interviews were based on a semi-structured questionnaire designed largely as a means of confirming the responses from the in-depth interviews. The key issues to be covered were agreed by H&B.

The open questions included such as:

"Whether you have had dealings with Healey & Baker or not, what is your general impression of Healey & Baker?"

And the structured questions such as:

"How would you rate Healey & Baker on a scale 1-5, where 5 indicates excellent and 1 indicates poor, on the following characteristics:

A.   It is progressive and forward-thinking

F.   Has good internal co-ordination

H.   Strong research team

I.   Maintains good client contact"

Results

The research was successfully concluded and took 10 weeks from initial agency selection, through briefing, sampling and methodology agreement, questionnaire design, Stage 1 fieldwork, analysis, Stage 2 questionnaire design and fieldwork, analysis, and final report.

The study fulfilled its required aims in identifying for Healey & Baker a number of issues to tackle. Some of them entailed reshaping the way it offered services to clients and these are covered in Case Study 3 at the end of Chapter 5, Adapting.

Chapter 5

Marketing in practice: Adapting

Chapter 2 explained that the working process that is marketing entailed first Finding Out all about clients' needs: how, when, where they might want a product or service and how much it was worth to them; then Adapting to provide products or services to fit these needs – at a profit. This Adapting bit of marketing – Product Development in professional marketing terms – is, as already suggested, much tougher within a service supplier than in a company making tangible products.

What do we adapt?

In practice this is the least developed aspect of marketing, not just within the commercial property sector, but in professional services generally. Too often when it is done the process of adapting is undertaken outside the marketing department. Perhaps not surprisingly, even those marketing textbooks that have been written to date within professional services have not fully covered this aspect of marketing. Yet this is the very core of marketing – changing to meet client needs.

One of the very best examples in recent years of Adapting within the service sector is that of Direct Line Insurance, when an entirely new company was born in 1985 on the back of a marketing idea. In essence, the personal motor insurance business, before Direct Line, lived on the premise that the strong supported the weak – the low-risk customers subsidised the high-risk ones.

Direct Line recognised that much good business could be won by pricing more keenly to lower risk clients. The new residential based demographic systems (ACORN, Mosaic, Pinpoint) developed in the early 1980s allowed for the more sophisticated targeting and underwriting needed. Competition among telecom companies also pushed down the cost of telephone generated business and, by offering their service direct and cutting out the middle-man, Direct Line were able to contain their cost base and price lower. The promotion to the most likely targets, of significant premium reductions by acting direct proved to be a winner. The inevitably "cleaner" book as a result enabled Direct Line to maintain its keen pricing. It soon added home contents insurance.

Other insurance companies were remarkably slow to react to this "cherry picking". The results for them were that they were losing their best business, with the higher risk business becoming an ever larger share, thus increasing their costs and ability to respond accordingly. All in all Direct Line had about seven years' start before, with much blood-letting, the industry responded. Direct Line's edge was eroded and the company has since moved into other markets, applying similar strategies to that used so successfully in the motor and house insurance markets.

It is not often, however. that the opportunity presents itself to launch a totally new concept. More often it is a question of adapting an existing service.

In Chapter 3 the example of a restaurant demonstrated that what the client buys is a complex service that has at its core the professional skill, with a whole range of other interactions around that core. This is the same with commercial property service providers and we need to address both.

Adapting the core professional skill

The core professional skill might be agency, designing, funding, auditing or whatever. This will be the raison d'être for the organisation's existence and it is unlikely that the organisation will survive for long if this core skill is not carried out with a certain degree of competence – at least within the market it operates.

Certain service suppliers within commercial property are in fact known to have particularly highly developed professional skills within certain areas. This may be the result of extensive experience in certain types of work, sheer weight of numbers and market knowledge, key individuals and so on. Such a reputation, which usually reflects judgement by fellow professionals, be they clients, competitors or media, is hard won and is to be protected as keenly as possible. Distinction by professional skill is highly desirable in that it gives genuine competitive advantage and, usually, carries premium pricing.

Adapting, or product development, may entail the introduction of a new professional service. Development of the service for the market should not be lead by the professional supplying the service, though they will of course have a critical input. Service development is best handled by people skilled in service development and this means marketing people. This is usually an activity undertaken within the organisation.

The object, for the service developer, is to bring all the requisite parts of the organisation to the point of accepting the service offer as meeting a perceived market need. This often entails much internal legwork, explanation, lobbying, cajoling even and is the unseen and unsung part of marketing. Typically the considerations that need to be embraced are:

Sales   Do those who will have to present the service to clients believe they have a winner? If not, what tuning would make it so?

Finance   Are the profitability projections sound? Is the cost base agreed? Will there be impact elsewhere?

Systems   Does the service entail any systems support? Does the database allow for the ready identification of use and users? Are client or management reports required?

Legal   Is the service allowed? Do any licences or approvals have to be obtained?

Insurance   Will the service have any impact on the organisation's cover, especially professional indemnity cover?

Personnel   Does the service require new staff positions, or realignment of existing duties? What training is needed for all staff likely to come into contact with the service?

Promotion Which promotional methods are earmarked to launch the service? Check availability of media. Timings both to deliver and to find the right market moment. Budget.

Approval for change

If all of the above issues are considered and the internal support obtained, then the project can be put with confidence to the board or management. They should demand a formal proposal that will give them confidence in approving the project. A suggested framework for the proposal paper might be:

1. What is the Committee being asked to approve,
    e.g. introduction of a new service/existing service in new market/adjustment of an existing service?

2. What is the service?

    — basic features

3. What market(s) does it service, supported by research?

    — how does the market split?
    — what benefits are sought by sector?
    — how is the market identified/accessed?
    — what is the size of the market?

4. How does the service meet the benefits sought?

    — what are the competing services?
    — what are the unique selling points of our service?

5. Launch methodology

    — delivery channels
    — type of promotional support
    — timings
    — sales force education

6. Profitability, supported by finance function

    — quantity and margin projections
    — cost projections

7. Fit

    – assurance of systems capability
    – assurance of legal approval
    – assurance of internal audit approval
    – assurance of personnel approval
    – assuming it is the marketing department putting forward
      the proposal, their approval can be taken as read.

Joint ventures

There will be occasions when a service is provided with the help
of a third party. In such cases the processes and the proposal to
management will be more complex. The respective roles of the
parties in the joint venture need to be spelt out clearly.
Management will need additional reassurance that the service
input by the partner organisation will be good enough and that
their reputation and mix of business do not create any difficulties.
The agreement between the organisations will need to set out
where responsibilities begin and end and, in the event of
disappointing performance in the market of either the service or
one of its providers, just what processes will come into effect to
protect the positions both of clients and service suppliers.

Delivering the service

In general the above product or service development process
should apply to the launch of a service or to any new marketing
initiative. It could, for example, be used to assess and propose
entry into a new market, or internal restructuring to meet a
market's needs better.

   With any service sector it is not simply a question of deciding
upon the features of a service and then launching or relaunching it
to the market. With a tangible product the correct tooling and
production processes are put in place to ensure that each copy of
that product is identical and delivers the promise that is offered.
Service companies need to do the same.

   As already discussed this cannot, in a professional service,
mean replicating the service exactly among different individuals.
What it must mean, however, is guaranteeing a minimum standard
of performance regardless of the individual member of staff

providing the service. Professional service companies need to "tool up" to deliver minimum quality levels.

Quality control can be effected in a number of different ways, all of which need to be utilised to "guarantee" performance. Recruiting and keeping quality staff has to be the start point. I do not allude only to professional property staff, as increasingly organisations in the property sector are recognising the need to have a broader range of skills even to deliver core professional services.

Recruiting staff should have been easier during the 1990s but competition for the very best staff has remained keen, even though the scale of recruitment is reduced. The need for quality therefore is recognised. At recruitment stage, and certainly beyond, good trainees will expect to see a programme of training and development that will grow their professional skills and afford them job satisfaction and opportunities for career advancement.

It is very much in the employer's interests to provide such training and development. Quite apart from the need to retain the sort of staff that will enhance the organisation's service and reputation, it ensures that the quality of the service delivered is kept high and the likelihood of legal action by a client for non-or under-performance is reduced. Most companies in the sector have now developed programmes that embrace on-the-job training and a range of sessions for Continuous Professional Development.

All staff, no matter how good or well-trained they are will make mistakes from time to time, particularly in the early years of their careers. Employers need therefore to have "safety nets" in place to catch the mistakes before they impact externally. Increasing attention has been given to quality control in recent years to preserve service standards, avoid claims and minimise professional indemnity cover. Procedures manuals, set approval processes and on-going supervision by senior staff are all important formal safety nets; while open plan offices and the chance to discuss issues with colleagues informally also help to avoid errors and develop skills.

It follows that whenever a new service is being proposed all of these quality control considerations need to be addressed to ensure that, from the day the service is launched, it is delivering the promise it is making.

There have been comparatively few genuinely new services in the property market in recent years, but I anticipate that we are about to see more. The heavy investment in IT within the sector has already brought with it some new professional services : computer aided design, lease management systems, information services such as EGi and Property Link.

Market segmentation

Through the superior intelligence about the market that the IT developments will offer, and also through the more sophisticated market segmentation that it will allow, service suppliers will be much better able to determine who needs what and to deliver it. Chapter 7 will return to segmentation, looking at marketing within the business plan. Since it is potentially a rich source for service development ideas, it is appropriate to establish here what is meant by market segmentation.

Segmentation is looking at markets as being made up of groupings of clients that have common characteristics. These common characteristics may be geographical, demographical, psychographical, by size, by type, by behaviour. Without in any way reducing the significance of each client within the segment, grouping them in this way is a valuable means of targeting.

For a market segment to be viable as a target it must be:

Measurable

Unless the segment can be quantified separately in terms of its trading potential, it will not be possible to assess whether it is worth targeting in the first place or to measure the success of doing so subsequently.

Homogenous

Unless the clients within the segment are sufficiently similar and likely to react in similar ways, there is unlikely to be any means of meeting their needs with a common service offer or appealing to them in a common way.

As already suggested, they also need to identify themselves readily by the characteristics that make them homogenous. Within the property sector, clients might well respond to being labelled "developers", "chartered surveyors" or "pension funds", but who naturally responds to being labelled "tenants" even though they might well be tenants. They are much more likely to think of themselves as printers, Londoners, exporters, etc.

Large enough.

Obviously a segment that is too small to warrant special attention is not going to be viable, though what is viable will vary from one service supplier to another.

Accessible.

There is little point in formulating a grouping of clients if they cannot be approached as that group. In the property sector a grouping that would be an attractive target segment for a number of service suppliers might be "companies whose property assets constitute more than 30% of their total assets". Regrettably though, they are not identifiable as a grouping (not that I have found anyway, if somebody else has, I would like to hear from them!).

The whole point of segmenting the market is to identify limited numbers of clients that can be serviced and promoted to in a more focused, cost-effective way. Segmentation should be applied at the commencement of the marketing process – at the Finding out stage. Where analysis and research suggests a segment could be profitably targeted it may well be appropriate to develop a service or package of services aimed at that sector.

In practice, most firms in the property sector do offer certain service lines to different segments, but the amount of segmented promotion is limited. Given that the marketing of buildings is highly segmented it cannot be too long before we see more segmented service offers in the market. The professional skills at the core of the service package to one segment may not in practice be very different from another if the clients' needs are similar. This should not, however, inhibit service packaging for target segments – it is what the client perceives that counts. Every industry sector tends to think of itself as unique, with its own specialised problems and needs, and this should be acknowledged and catered for in service development.

The service the client buys

So far we have looked at the process of Adapting as it relates to launching new or adjusting the existing core professional services offered. In the restaurant example we looked at in Chapter 3, we saw though that clients select service suppliers on a much broader range of interactions than just the professional skill at the core of the service.

Nor should the other interactions in the service relationship be dismissed as merely secondary to the professional skill. Consider these two points: satisfaction and differentiation.

Consistently in market research studies undertaken in the commercial property sector, clients express satisfaction with the professional advice given or action taken, but dissatisfaction with the way they have been treated as clients. Common complaints have included: not keeping the client informed as the project progressed; not understanding the clients' broader business needs; non-availability of partners; poor fielding of telephone calls; overlong reports, etc. Clearly there is considerable room for improving client service in many areas other than the core professional skill.

Secondly, it is where service is at its most variable that clients will be best able to differentiate one firm from another. If the client believes that a similar level of core professional skill exists in each of the most likely service providers, then he or she will base his or her decision to appoint and retain suppliers on other, more variable factors.

Figure 4, on the following page, echoes the model of the restaurant and suggests what service issues might exist between, for example, a surveying firm and its client. Just as with the restaurant, different service aspects will have varying importance to different clients. A firm that waits for complaints to identify what matters is leaving things too late. Knowing precisely what is likely to appeal to each client is probably best left to each account handler, but formal research will identify a firm's stronger points and weaknesses and suggest areas for attention.

The first, obvious observation is that, just as with the restaurant there is a whole host of interactions between service supplier and client. Each of these interactions is an opportunity to impress or to disappoint the client. It follows that all service

Fig 4	The service product – surveyor

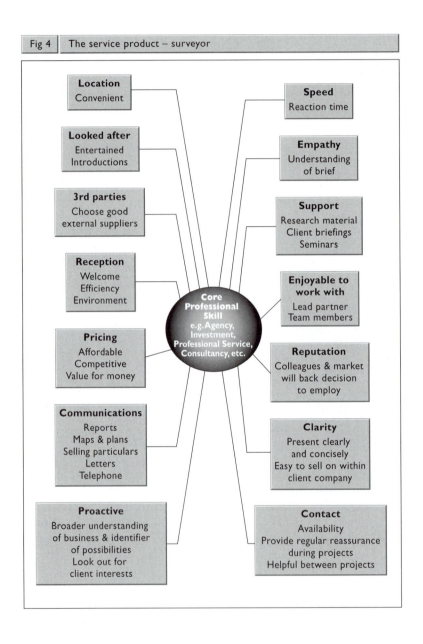

Location
Convenient

Speed
Reaction time

Looked after
Entertained
Introductions

Empathy
Understanding
of brief

3rd parties
Choose good
external suppliers

Support
Research material
Client briefings
Seminars

Reception
Welcome
Efficiency
Environment

**Enjoyable to
work with**
Lead partner
Team members

**Core
Professional
Skill**
e.g. Agency,
Investment,
Professional Service,
Consultancy, etc.

Pricing
Affordable
Competitive
Value for money

Reputation
Colleagues & market
will back decision
to employ

Communications
Reports
Maps & plans
Selling particulars
Letters
Telephone

Clarity
Present clearly
and concisely
Easy to sell on within
client company

Proactive
Broader understanding
of business & identifier
of possibilities
Look out for
client interests

Contact
Availability
Provide regular reassurance
during projects
Helpful between projects

organisations need to address performance in all these areas if they wish to impress rather than disappoint. With competition fierce and differentiation between core professional skills perhaps limited it could be under- performance in just one of these total service interactions that will enable a client to distinguish between firms and go elsewhere.

One of the interactions on the chart, pricing, is obviously an important one and one that all marketing textbooks cite as a critical element for marketing people to control. There is no doubt that pricing can make all the difference. My own experience in financial services with "free banking" for current accounts, as well as the Direct Line example already discussed are good examples. For every example of pricing being the determining factor, however, there are other examples of it not being so. All people do not buy their food in the cheapest local supermarket, nor do they invest in the life assurance companies which come at the top of the league tables for sums realised for money invested.

Research among corporate buyers consistently shows that, while they may be more objective than consumers at large, they too are persuaded by motivations other than price. Quality of service, however defined, is the paramount consideration and, generally, clients are prepared to pay extra to get better service. Indeed, low pricing may put buyers off in the belief that they are unlikely to get the level of service they require if the price is set low. The implications for pricing, therefore, are to understand competitor pricing levels and pitch your offer accordingly – consistent with the quality of service you are able to demonstrate. Raising service standards allows latitude in pricing.

All staff are involved

The other clear message from the chart is that the relationship between client and supplier, again just like the restaurant, depends upon a wide range of staff. Some of the interactions, other than provision of the core professional skill, are carried out by the "professional" staff. Many, however, depend upon the other staff, often labelled within our sector as "support" staff. Indeed, ultimately every single person working for a service organisation affects to varying degrees the level and style of service offered.

The implications of this are that all job functions need to be looked at in the light of client attitude studies. All staff need to know what it is that impresses and what it is that disappoints. They then need to be given the resources to deliver impressive, not disappointing performance. By resources I mean the time, the clear remit, the training, the environment, the equipment, the budget possibly and the feedback. Encouragingly, many organisations in the sector have recognised the need to improve this total service.

First and foremost, perhaps if staff are to offer a revised service they need to be given the remit and the time to discharge it. Professional service firms of all types often lack the courage of their convictions and compromise by asking staff to overlay new duties onto existing roles. Increasingly though, specialist roles are being created to provide specialist advice e.g. corporate services. (*see illustration on page 71*)

Similarly, it has been recognised that account handling takes time and particular attention. The mix of skills required is different for instance from that needed to win new business, and within any organisation some individuals will be better suited to the one role than the other. In either case there is a clear need to plan the role, consider the activities required throughout the budget period, and co-ordinate these to the client's benefit. (This will be covered in more detail in Chapter 7.)

Helping staff to perform

In recent years much more attention has been given to training all staff in client care. In particular, training has been extended to those staff who, in less enlightened times, used to be called 'support staff'. Abandoning this designation, with its derogatory implications, demonstrates a more mature appreciation of the way a service organisation interacts with its clients. At a stroke, it also encourages all those members of staff to recognise that they too have a role to play in the relationship and a responsibility to help deliver the promise. Many so-called "support staff" such as receptionists, telephonists and secretaries are in the front line of client contact.

For those supplying the core professional skills too, training has been introduced to help them understand better how the advice they give clients actually assists clients in their overall business objectives. Only by understanding the client's own business needs can any "professional" truly look out for their client's best interests and be proactive in proposing solutions and opportunities. This role entails a broader business understanding than has been required traditionally.

A supportive environment ought to be a well understood notion in the commercial property sector. Many organisations have in fact reconfigured their space in recent years to supply entrance, reception and presentational facilities that are more likely to make a positive impression on clients.

Research studies into modern office practices list an impressive range of equipment that workers now expect to have at their disposal. The property sector is no exception and many organisations have invested heavily to upgrade the quality of their kit. This ranges across information provision on screen, through communication tools, to presentational equipment. The combined effect is to enhance significantly the knowledge, advice and speed of response that can be given to clients.

Presentational material is another area that has seen significant improvements in recent years. The content and quality of reports and brochures is, at its best, very good, though there is still too much routine material whose role is not clear. This will be looked at in more detail in the next chapter. The provision of good material is helpful in maintaining the contact, advice and support that clients increasingly expect from a relationship.

The reader may feel that some of the issues listed above are simply common-sense management issues and that organisations naturally generate such improvements anyway without calling it marketing. This may well be the case and certainly the thrust for improving client service or staff performance should not come only from the marketing function. The marketing process demands, however, that whatever Adapting is effected, be it a core professional service or one of the many client/firm interactions layered around it, that satisfaction of client's needs – profitably – be the driving motivation. This too is much more likely to be achieved if it is done in a co-ordinated way, to which all service suppliers within the organisation are committed.

On the assumption that the organisation has assessed market requirements, identified targets and adapted its service provision to meet those requirements profitably, it will be ready to tell the market.

Exercise 1 : Are you close to your customers?

I have yet to meet an organisation that will admit to not being close to its customers. Yet few have truly adapted themselves to follow through what being client-led really means. The Service Management Partnership has prepared this exercise to help you judge for yourself where your organisation stands.

1. Do staff who come into contact with customers understand the company's goals and its marketing objectives?

A	B	C	D	E
Totally	Extensively	Reasonably	Partly	Not at all
❑	❑	❑	❑	❑

2. Do staff support what the company stands for and identify with its values?

A	B	C	D	E
Yes	Probably	Maybe	Unlikely	No
❑	❑	❑	❑	❑

3. Do your plans for new services specifically include the role of staff and your expectations of them as part of the service specifications?

A	B	C	D	E
Always	Usually	Sometimes	Seldom	Never
❑	❑	❑	❑	❑

4. Do job roles and specifications – even for Head Office staff – specify their relationship to customers – albeit within a chain of contact internally?

A	B	C	D	E
Always	Largely	Sometimes	Seldom	Never
❑	❑	❑	❑	❑

5. Suppose a customer were to complain about an aspect of your service to a member of staff – who found himself/herself agreeing strongly with the criticism. What do you think the staff member would do?

A	B	C	D	E
Help them make a complaint	Listen attentively	Smile & agree	Ignore it	Say, "it's not my problem"
❑	❑	❑	❑	❑

6. When a customer complains do you think that staff's reaction – the manner in which the complaint would be handled – would leave the customer believing that his/ her complaint was:

A	B	C	D	E
Important?	Of concern?	Being dealt with?	Of no concern?	Don't know?
❏	❏	❏	❏	❏

7. Clearly efforts will be made to resolve complaints, but are complaints used for quality-control purposes too?

A	B	C	D	E
Always	Usually	Sometimes	Never	Don't Know
❏	❏	❏	❏	❏

8. Targets/budgets are often set against products and services. Are your targets set against customer types and segments?

A	B	C	D	E
Always	Largely	Partly	Sometimes	Never
❏	❏	❏	❏	❏

9. Do you communicate with staff – on a 2-way basis – about your/their understanding of the market and its needs?

A	B	C	D	E
Always	Usually	Largely	Seldom	Never
❏	❏	❏	❏	❏

10. Do customer contact staff receive formal training in dealing with customers?

A	B	C	D	E
Regularly	As necessary	Sometimes	Rearely	Never
❏	❏	❏	❏	❏

Score 4 for any A box, 3 for B, 2 for C, 1 for D and 0 for E.

If you can honestly score 30 or more you are close to your customers.

If you score less than 10 it may be too late!

If you score between 10 and 30 it may help to consider some remedial activity to improve your situation.

Case study 2: Changing the culture

In Chapter 2 we talked about a natural resistance, within professional service organisations, to changing working practices. Inevitably this limits the degree to which a firm can be truly responsive to clients' needs. Tackling this issue entails a fundamental shift in culture, which takes both time and effort. This though is what top 10 law firm Simmons & Simmons took on.

Although this case study is from a different sector, the parallels with commercial property organisations are sufficiently clear for the study to be relevant.

Background

Simmons & Simmons had grown rapidly throughout the 1980s and by 1992 had 121 partners and 224 assistants, and was making good profits. Under the previous senior partner, partners had been free to develop business in an opportunistic way and this had proved successful. Then the recession struck.

New managing partner, Alasdair Neil, recognised that the firm was not well equipped to deal with the recession and compete effectively on an international scale. Internally, the management structure was weak and not providing direction, and communications were poor. Externally, the image was of a firm dominated by a few equity partners. Above all, the firm needed a strategy and the structure to deliver it. In 1993 Alasdair Neil brought in consultants Hodgart-Temporal to assist.

The programme

Hodgart-Temporal worked with the firm for the next 18 months. Their involvement covered three stages: research, strategy discussions, and implementation.

Research

The research into how the firm was perceived was carried out among clients and staff. Of the firm's top 50 clients, 25 were interviewed and a consistent pattern of response emerged. Individual professional skills were praised, but clients did not feel they knew other parts of the firm or what they had to offer. Partners were used to running their own client stables independently.

The staff interviews voiced frustration and disappointment and a feeling of being remote from management. These problems were found to be widespread. Alan Hodgart reported the findings back to the partners early in 1994 and, though surprised at the extent of the problems, to their great credit the partners accepted the findings and approved moving to the next stage of the programme.

Strategy discussions

The second stage consisted of a series of strategy discussions over three months. The discussions, led by Alan Hodgart, entailed a considerable investment by the firm. All of the partners, in groups of 10 and across functions, met for six-hour workshops to discuss the way the firm was organised and where it should be going.

Hodgart-Temporal analysed the results of the findings and drew up the main choices facing the firm. These were presented to the equity partners in October 1994 at a weekend conference at Keble College, Oxford. The report was well received, even by those who had doubted the process of using management consultants. The conference went on the following day to make recommendations on a wide range of issues: international strategy; targeting; management restructuring; account responsibility; and training.

Implementation

The management of the firm was swiftly restructured. All departments chose their managing partners and the firm's management committee, entitled the Operations Committee, was formed. It comprised the managing heads of departments including, for the first time, finance, marketing, personnel and IT.

A separate strategy and policy committee was elected. Only the managing partner sits on both committees. In response to the experience cited by clients, cross-functional client management teams were established for the firm's major clients, and client management plans written.

The final stage in the programme was the preparation of a three-year business plan for the firm and for each of the legal departments. This again was an intensive exercise over several months, but in October 1995, the plan was proposed and accepted at a partner meeting. The firm's international strategy was subsequently agreed at a partners' weekend.

The result

The process of re-inventing itself took the firm the best part of two years. It entailed a considerable input of time and effort, and indeed the cost of employing the management consultancy.

Within Simmons & Simmons the change in culture has been almost tangible. The clear direction provided now and the opportunity, through group discussion, to discuss and contribute to the business plan has generated a fundamentally different atmosphere. As Alasdair Neil says: "That's the point of all these structures and meetings; it's the way you get the input, the enthusiasm, the ideas, the intelligence of all your people."

This culture change is now beginning to make its impact in the market. One of the first effects has been on recruitment. The firm now finds it easier to attract good people in for interviews and to employ them. Already too, the message is getting through to clients, as a survey of a sample of clients has demonstrated.

Case study 3: Adapting by using research

Case Study 1 outlined the research study undertaken by Healey & Baker in 1989 among clients and non-clients. Having covered that Finding out process, this study explains the Adapting Healey & Baker put in hand in the light of the findings.

Just three topics are selected from the findings to demonstrate how, when the will exists, research can be the catalyst for improving performance.

Promoting the entity of the firm

Various findings suggested the firm would benefit from more co-ordinated promotion:

> While clients stressed the importance of individual — usually Partner contact, their loyalty was ultimately to the firm;

> Having a "department" is equated with having the necessary specialist knowledge, but it also suggests to clients narrow vision and a breakdown in internal communication;

> Like the other firms covered in the survey, H&B was given a poor rating for "good internal co-ordination".

H&B reaction

At that time each department had its own marketing budget and produced its own material. As a result they seemed like different organisations, with no concerted benefit for the large amounts being spent. The research prompted the firm to unify the marketing budget centrally and to promote the firm rather than individual departments.

All promotional activity since has been focused on client types with the range of services presented. This has extended to the multi-disciplinary teams formulated for assisting individual clients.

The result has been a more unified delivery of service and an improved cross-selling record, together with a stronger profile in the market for the firm in total. A subsidiary benefit has been, in putting the budget within the control of the marketing department, the money has been spent to better effect.

Client contact

All firms were described as weak at maintaining contact with clients.

H&B reaction

All partners were urged to take care to keep clients informed of progress throughout a project; to guard against the tendency to delegate work; and to adopt a closer duty of care to their clients.

In support, the client mailing system was overhauled, and a regular programme of client newsletters and research publications generated to maintain communication, brief clients on market developments and promote the range of services and offices.

Corporate identity

The survey said that the firm's visual image was of a traditional, highly professional firm, but at the same time slow and old-fashioned. Clients, who knew the firm, pointed out that the visual image was lagging behind the reality of the firm's lively, on-the-ball personality. Non-clients believed the outdated image.

H&B reaction

The corporate identity was changed. This ranged across all printed material and promotional work. The implications of the findings were, however, taken much further. The firm's premises were changed: a new display frontage, reception area, and conference suite was created to present a more modern business-like environment, and staffing and equipment acquired for them. New standards were set for written communications and new training programmes set up for reception, switchboard and secretarial staff. All equipment was programmed to output to the new standards.

The research findings, warts and all, were presented to the entire staff of the firm and the programmes being adopted were spelt out. It was made clear that the visual identity was merely the expression of the firm's personality and that the performance which defined that personality was the responsibility of all.

The exercise was received very positively by all staff and the consistent image established reflects a much higher degree of consistency and co-ordination of effort throughout the firm.

Paul Orchard-Lisle of Healey & Baker receiving the
Queen's Award for Export Achievement 1996 from the Lord Lieutenant
of Greater London, Field Marshal the Lord Bramall. See page 6.

2. The range of research undertaken by the leading firms of surveyors
gets increasingly sophisticated. See page 31.

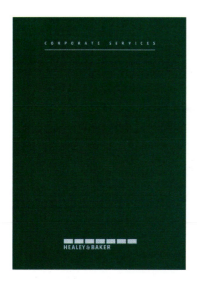

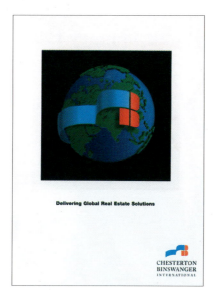

3. Corporate Real Estate Services is one example of how surveying
firms are genuinely adapting to meet client needs. See page 60.

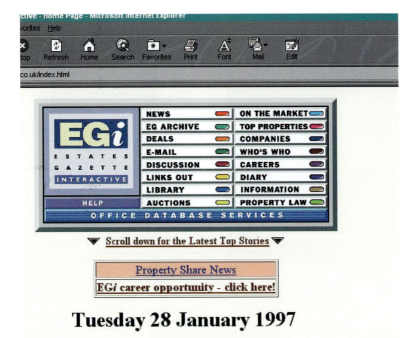

EGi – the interactive information service launched mid 1996 by the
Estates Gazette. See pages 100-101.

Knight Frank's corporate identity manual which won the Special Judges'
Award in the UK Property Marketing Awards 1995. See pages 102-4

HEALEY & BAKER

Branding has become recognised as an important marketing tool. Most of the leading firms of surveyors have addressed this issue in recent years.

JLW washes whiter! Top, the successful sponsorship of cleaning statues
in the Parc Royal, Brussels; below, before and after shots of the statue
of St. Nepornuck, Luxembourg. See pages 105-6

8. The highest profile advertising in the industry is celebrated at the
Estates Gazette front cover awards

9.
International
exhibitions such as
MAPIC shown
here attract
organisations from
all sides of the
industry.

10. The UK Property Marketing Awards each year encourage the
standards of marketing practice in the industry.

Chapter 6

Marketing in practice: Communicating

Telling the market, through marketing communications, about the company and its products or services is, by definition, the most visible part of marketing. Almost every waking moment of our lives we are each exposed to promotional messages from one direction or another. It is hardly surprising, therefore, that most people think marketing means promotion.

Edward Cleaveley wrote in 1983: "In the property profession there is a great deal of confusion about the meaning of promotion, the most common error in my experience being the use of the term 'marketing' instead of 'promotion'."[1]. It must be said that the confusion persists. This does not help those endeavouring to practise marketing. As Neil Morgan said in 1990: "The prevailing typology of marketing as 'advertising and selling' with its allied ignorance of the nature of marketing, causes professional services marketers more problems than anything else".[2]

There are two main problems this causes for professional marketing people. The first is that many people (and not just property professionals), consider that they know something about marketing communications. Being exposed to promotion themselves as consumers, as well as to promotional activities relating to property, they believe they are experts. The fact that their professional examinations have included some elements of marketing communications exacerbates this. The second is that they do not usually recognise communicating as the third stage in the marketing process after Finding out and Adapting. The upshot is that marketing communications are often approached in an unstructured and subjective way. This leads to poor briefing and to prejudiced assessment of recommendations.

In Chapter 3 I said that marketing people see the Communicating activities within the context of a business development aim and judge each activity on its ability to meet a particular need. The earlier stages of target identification and understanding, and the shaping of the offer to meet their needs, render the selection of communication tools very much more straightforward. There is a broad range of such tools at the disposal of the marketing professional and each has its particular strengths and appropriateness for use just like the tools in a domestic toolbox.

Broadly, the tools available for approaching the market are:

1.	Sales force	4.	Sponsorship
	— Own		
	— Third party	5.	Brochures
2.	Advertising	6.	Direct marketing
	— Press		
	— Broadcast	7.	Seminars and conferences
	— Outdoor		
		8.	Exhibitions
3.	Public Relations		
	— Media	9.	Promotional items
	— Public		

Before we look at these tools, however, we should look at the Communicating processes that should come in advance of a full-scale approach to the market: internal communication and test marketing.

Internal communication

We have seen that so much of the service offer depends upon the staff who, in their varied roles and client interactions, deliver the service. Staff feedback too is a vital part of the Finding out about client needs and attitudes to the service provided. It follows that any new market or service initiative must have the full understanding and support of staff if it is to succeed.

In Chapter 5, Adapting, we saw how a new initiative should be discussed with the various functions of the organisation to ensure it is shaped appropriately. The conceptual support of staff should be forthcoming if it is explained that they, or colleagues like them, have played a part in formulating the initiative. Staff should be made aware how the initiatives will benefit the organisation and ultimately of course themselves.

Converting this conceptual support into the positive action required to achieve success will depend on a number of factors. Staff will also need to feel:

- they are helping their clients
- they fully understand the service and market
- they appreciate the role they will have to play
- they have the time to deliver
- they have the supporting resources to make an impact
- their efforts will be monitored and rewarded.

Each of these issues has to be addressed. The first three are essentially issues of communication which can be met by: internal conferences; team briefings; individual training; individual sales packs; in-house newsletters or a combination of these. Being given the time to deliver their required role should have been addressed in the Adapting stage of the marketing process. If staff say "When am I going to be able to do this?" or "What about the rest of my work?" then the prospects for success of the new initiative are limited.

In addition to the precious resource of time, the facility to use that time effectively will depend upon the level of supporting resources supplied. These will range from equipment to assist working processes, to information services to boost intelligence, to promotional support to render selling activities easier and more effective (see below).

The final point listed above, monitoring and rewarding, is not to suggest simply a response to the crude "What's in this for me?". In my experience, service industry employees are more public spirited and well-motivated than employers sometimes give credit for. There is a natural interest to see results of efforts, both individually and collectively, and to work on the necessary adjustments to get it right next time. In fact, there are few things that give staff a bigger lift than their employer demonstrating its preparedness to learn lessons in the market-place and adapt accordingly.

Internal communication does take time and therefore there is a cost entailed. It is, however, an investment that should pay back handsomely. If an organisation does not communicate its aims –

broad or specific – to the staff who deliver them, it is only a matter of time before somebody in some part of the organisation 'drops the ball'. It may be on a general service matter rather than the core professional service, but the impression will be given of an organisation that hasn't got its act together. This creates doubt in the mind of the client, and risks undermining the relationship.

Test marketing

In Chapter 2 we saw that, after launching a new initiative in the market, response tracking in effect takes us back to the Finding out stage, which might generate further service Adapting. Hopefully, if the research and analysis has been sound, the service adaptation well executed and the subsequent promotion effective, then the venture should succeed. But there is always a risk that at some stage something has been overlooked or one of the processes not carried out carefully enough. Equally, market requirements can shift, competitors can respond. The result can be a very expensive failure.

Cost is incurred at all stages in the marketing process. In manufacturing industries the greatest investment might come at the Adapting stage. The development of a new product in the aerospace or motor industry may entail the investment of hundreds of millions of pounds over several years. The same is true of course with a new property development. For professional service suppliers, though, the greatest cost is more likely to be incurred at the promotional stage. It is therefore highly attractive to obtain a measure of the market's likely reaction before embarking on full-scale promotion.

Test marketing is, as the name implies, a process of launching an initiative in a restricted way and testing the reaction. The test may be a restriction to a few, hand-picked clients; it may be a restriction to a geographical area or a single market segment; it may be only part of the envisaged service. The aim is the same: to reduce the risk inherent in doing something new.

The test allows for mistakes to be made but on a limited scale, so that corrections can be made before full promotion. This is particularly valuable if the service is a new concept and market reaction that much more difficult to determine. Answers to "What if...?" type questions in market research always need to be treated with care and further testing.

It should also be said that there are disadvantages in test marketing. There is inevitably a certain cost of time and money in carrying out the test. Time is likely to be the more critical since it delays the moment when the service suppliers can take advantage of the market opportunity it has seen. It may be that delay is not sustainable.

The other risk is that the organisation is breaking cover and competitors will see the new initiative. Some companies go to considerable lengths to test new products in as isolated circumstances as possible in the hope of escaping broader public, and competitor notice. (Because of its remoteness geographically, Hull used to be favoured by consumer goods companies as a test marketing area.)

There is obviously a balance to be struck between wishing to get the initiative as right as possible before public launch and the delay and cost of testing. Where testing will tend to be most advisable is when a conceptually new service is being launched and likely market reaction is more difficult to gauge. In such circumstances a longer lead time between testing and ultimate launch should be planned to allow for adjustments in the service as a result of lessons learned from the test marketing.

See Case study 4 – Test Marketing: EGi

Selecting the promotional tools

Just like the tools in a domestic toolbox, the various means of promotion are each good at particular tasks. The marketing professional will therefore select the appropriate tool for the job. Like most domestic jobs too, many marketing tasks require a combination of tools if they are to be accomplished successfully.

The fundamental questions to pose in order to determine which promotional tools to employ are:

1.   Who do we want to communicate with?

2.   What do we seek to achieve?

3.   How much is it worth to us to effect the communication?

1.   Who do we want to communicate with?

This should be readily apparent from the Finding out process already undertaken. Targets may be potential clients, existing clients, introducers of clients, staff or a combination of these. For all of the promotional tools listed at the beginning of this chapter targets can either be selected (e.g. sales force calls, mailings, conference invitations) or are implicit (e.g. Granada viewers, *Financial Times* readers). Whilst "Granada viewers" or "FT readers" may sound vague and unhelpful, in practice media are regularly audited in terms of their audience and comprehensive breakdowns of audiences are readily available from a range of media research organisations. From this data media planners can make ready comparisons between competing media. The competing media, too, use such comparisons to support their case. The *Financial Times* for instance can demonstrate its readership in a variety of ways. There are the standard demographic breakdowns you might expect, job title breaks, and the distribution of readership geographically. But there are also more tightly relevant comparisons available, such as chief executive officers, or senior executives responsible for property decisions, or executives making at least three business flights a year. The answer for media planners is to explain to the potential media which target audience they are trying to hit and let them respond, making their case. Be precise in your targeting. For example, applying a company size filter will produce different figures. Also check what media tell you with an independent media consultant.

The *Financial Times* can demonstrate how it compares with all its leading rivals in terms of coverage and cost for the target audience. It is then more flexible in what it can offer than most people imagine. Space can be bought in different issues around the world, advertisements can be varied around the world and greater precision can be obtained by utilising surveys which attract specialist readerships, or loose inserts, which can be broken down even to individual postcode regions.

Such precision in information and targeting does render the task of campaign planning easier. With all of the tools, therefore, the fitness for purpose in terms of targeting can readily be seen. This is not to suggest that all of the audience of any particular promotional method or media has to be a target. With all of the tools used there is a degree of wastage, as with most corporate assets. The strengths and weaknesses of each tool are covered below.

2. What do we seek to achieve?

This will depend on the state of the existing relationship between the supplier and the target. This entails understanding the nature of the **consumer buying process**. All consumers move through progressive stages before buying:

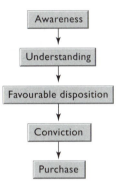

This applies to all consumers, private or business, and to all products and services. The time spent on each level of the buying process, however, may vary considerably, usually depending on the product or service being acquired. For example, we might move very quickly through all the levels of the buying process in the case of a newly launched chocolate product. We happen to be queuing at the supermarket checkout, spot the bar of chocolate on display and, almost before we know it, we've popped it into the trolley. Such "impulse purchases" tend to be made when the product is more peripheral to our basic living needs.

Much more care, time and persuasion is needed for people to change products related to security, health and hygiene, or finance. Consumers are much less willing, for example, to change their toothpaste or their bank. Large items of e tend to require a slower progress through the lev process. We need to feel that much more certain the 'right' decision before buying.

At any one time we are all at differing levels of the buying process for a whole host of goods and services. Much of what we buy is simply a repetition of previous purchases – we are already aware of the product, understand it, are favourably disposed towards it and convinced we will buy it again. Until a future purchase disappoints us, or we become aware of, understand and like an alternative product, the existing supplier is not threatened. Even for items we do not anticipate buying, or may never buy, we may be well advanced through the buying process. A Rolls-Royce or a Ferrari is known to most, understood by most, attractive to most. We may even be convinced we will buy just as soon as career progress, inheritance or lottery win allows. In the meantime, most of us will have to set our sights a little lower, but the enviable position Rolls-Royce and Ferrari find themselves in is a direct result of the reputations that they have worked hard to build and maintain over many decades.

The same principles apply in commercial property. At any time a service supplier will have attained varying levels of the buying process with each potential client in the market. A new service, by definition, starts with nil awareness and therefore no understanding of what the service offers, nor any motivation to buy. The same applies to a new company. An existing company with a new name also moves overnight to nil awareness and, though it should be able to build up through the levels of customer persuasion more quickly, it will have to start again at the awareness level.

In practice, of course, most organisations have: a body of existing clients who are at the Purchase level; other existing clients who are convinced but sometimes buy from a competitor; "warm" prospects who are favourably disposed but not yet clients; and a whole mass of potential targets who are only at the understanding, awareness or ignorance levels.

Knowing who is at what stage should have been part of any company's Finding out process (Chapter 4). Chapter 7 will look at the implications of this for the business plan, but at this stage we shall concentrate on the promotional implications for an individual service.

It is self-evident that, unless the initial Awareness level has been attained, then no company is going to sell anything. This level though is not addressed as vigorously within commercial property as in other sectors. Partly it may be that a certain amount of property dealing is done within fairly closely defined circles (e.g. development, investment). Given that many players are indeed well known within these circles, they maybe do not appreciate that they are much less well known outside in the general commercial world, which is also their market.

It is also the case that those promotional activities that are particularly good at raising awareness levels (advertising, sponsorship, exhibitions) tend to be less capable of moving customers the final stage into Purchase (where, for example, the sales force is a better tool). Such activities tend to be undervalued because the need to raise awareness is not fully appreciated. Yet, how many of us have been told, even by existing clients "Oh, I didn't know you: had an office in X / dealt with such and such property / offered a Y service..."?

A further point should be made in relation to Awareness. Studies have shown that we tend naturally to link quality with awareness. In other words we are more likely to think a company or product is good, the better known they are. "Never heard of them" is used as a derogatory remark. Similarly when recruiting, we are more likely to lean towards the individual who has worked for organisations we have heard of – even though this may mean the experience will have been more junior and less meaningful.

In business-to-business marketing there is generally a higher level of Understanding and market knowledge among purchasers, who are likely themselves to be professional. Unless, therefore, the service is conceptually new (e.g. chartered surveying in many countries outside the UK) or known not to be properly understood by clients (e.g. corporate asset management at boardroom level) then this stage – raising Understanding – should not require as much promotional effort as the Awareness and Persuasion stages. Curiously though, until quite recently, many brochures and client pitches in the commercial property sector laboriously went through the processes entailed in delivering the service as if the client did not understand the service.

Encouraging potential clients into having a favourable disposition is not simply a question of demonstrating one's own abilities, but also one's strengths competitively. Almost all of the promotional tools can assist at this stage (see strengths and weaknesses list below). Here we are looking to differentiate the company or service from, and promote its superiority over, its competitors. This is most unlikely to be achieved if the target audience does not know of the existence of the company or service, nor understands what it can offer – it is simply asking too much of the audience.

To move from a favourable disposition to a conviction to use a service almost certainly requires a much closer, probably personal contact. Many of the tools do not have a role at this stage. The sales force and seminars are more likely to be effective here.

We identified earlier that a conviction to use may not secure a client's every purchase. While the personal relationships the sales force builds are probably the most significant factor in generating repeat buying, the other tools still have a role to play. All organisations depend on their reputation. This not only has to be gained, but maintained. If a client has not heard of a company for some time, he may feel it is no longer a key supplier, or has declined or even gone out of business.

Many in professional services would argue that reputation is critical. It is of course an elusive concept that cannot be pinned down and measured. Nor can it be directly bought. What can be bought though, with promotional tools, are activities that develop, support and sustain reputation. Many of the promotional tools can contribute to reputation: sales force, media comment, advertising, sponsorship, conferences and seminars.

Reputation is key, too, in recruiting and keeping the good quality staff that sustain service delivery. The internal audience is often not considered when mounting external promotional activities, but vigorous external promotion does lift morale and pride, which go hand in hand with reputation.

As well as winning new clients, a good reputation will encourage existing clients to take further services. The individual service buyer is less likely to be criticised by colleagues if he or she selects a supplier with a strong reputation. The tools then are used to confirm post-purchase, to reassure the client and to keep him or her at the conviction level of the buying process so that when the need arises again he or she naturally moves to purchase.

3. How much is it worth to effect the communication?

Any organisation would like 100 per cent spontaneous awareness in its target market, a comprehensive understanding of its services, and an endless supply of convinced prospects waiting to buy. The scale and quality of the work and the pricing latitude afforded would significantly enhance bottom-line performance. Unfortunately, such levels of awareness, understanding and conviction would take a very considerable promotional investment over a very long time. Even then it may not be achievable: because of competitor reaction; market resistance; or the product simply not matching the promotion.

With each marketing initiative, therefore, we need to ask also: how much is it worth to us to achieve our goal? In an extreme case, if the cost of reaching the target market and moving enough of it towards the purchase level of the buying process is too great, then the initiative should be rethought. In practice, an initiative is unlikely to reach this stage since a good marketing person would have been conscious very early on in the project that the promotional costs likely to be needed would be too great.

What is more usual is that the promotional tools have to be brought to bear in as cost- effective way as possible to achieve the goal. In other words, compromise is sometimes necessary in using scarce resources. As the table below shows, there is a fair degree of overlap in what the different tools can achieve. What we have also already recognised is that most tasks require more than one tool. The marketing professional will therefore assemble the tools and the intensity of their use to deliver the initiative's aims as well as possible within a sensible budget.

Using the different tools in harmony will produce the best results. I have heard the view expressed that such and such a promotional tool is better than another. This is nonsense – akin to saying the fax is better than the telephone. The point is that they each perform certain roles well and, probably, are each better for being used in concert.

This raises the question of measurement of effectiveness. We have arrived at the mix of marketing tools we believe is the best to deliver the specific purpose. It follows that we should measure the effectiveness of our efforts. This is not always a straightforward task, not least because the market may take some time to respond. It is also not always possible to judge which tool produced the goods when tools are used in harness. No salesman is likely to admit that their own efforts were only half the story and that the advertising, editorial, mailing and brochures deserve the other half of the credit.

Yet this can be the case. In my last company, Lloyds Bowmaker, the corporate asset finance sales force was very well trained, was enthusiastic and well managed. Each deal concluded, however, was taking on average 22 sales calls. With targeting, advertising to raise awareness and understanding, mailing, telemarketing, and brochures to build understanding and a favourable disposition, we gave the sales force a much healthier platform. Over three years we reduced the number of calls per deal from 22 to 7 and doubled the average deal size.

On a corporate scale, it is normal for an organisation to have several target markets and several goals it wishes to achieve. Some, by virtue of where the organisation already stands, will require less resource allocation than others. This may help determine which initiatives are pursued and therefore which tools are used.

An identified weakness might be the overall market awareness of an organisation. Let us assume that it is 30% among the target market and the company judges that to ensure a sufficiently robust platform for its sales force to operate from, it needs to raise basic awareness to 50% of the market. The best tools for raising awareness are advertising or sponsorship. Both, however, would be expensive for this goal to be achieved, certainly many tens of thousands of pounds over two or three years. Whether this is supportable will depend on each company, but few, I suspect, in the commercial property market could make a good business case for this. The result though is that the sales force has a tougher task because the market has not been moved far enough along the buying decision process. The sales force is therefore significantly less effective, though this is not generally seen as a cost because it is not measured, and is probably written off as part of "the tough market".

Strengths and weaknesses of promotional tools

Of course, each tool is capable of variable performance – there are good and bad advertisements, mailshots, press releases, salesmen and so on. The strengths and weaknesses cited here are as between the different marketing tools and help show some of the ways options might be selected.

Tool

Sales force – Strengths

— Very good at moving customers through the latter stages of the buying process – from favourably disposed to purchase;

— Very good at keeping existing purchasers at the conviction stage;

— Naturally provide market feedback (though this will need more objective confirmation);

— Efforts are measurable, over time;

— Own sales forces are more loyal and build better long-term relationships between employer and client;

— Third party or self-employed sales forces tend to be more efficient and more predictable, since they are paid only by results.

Sales force – Weaknesses

— Inefficient at the Awareness and Understanding stages of the buying process;

— A very expensive tool to recruit, train and maintain;

— A very wasteful resource – hit rate tends to be very low;

— Require significant resource of other staff, systems and machinery, and promotional tools;

— Require disciplined management to avoid unco-ordinated and unpredictable activity.

Advertising – Strengths

– Gets messages across to large audiences and is therefore good at the Awareness, Understanding, and Favourable disposition stages of the buying process (see Case Study 7: Nelson Bakewell);

– Completely controllable. This is bought space or airtime and what is communicated (within the bounds of the law, decency and the Advertising Standards Authority) is your choice;

– The very wide array of publications, programmes or locations enables a good degree of targeting;

– Except for radio, advertising has the advantage over editorial of the visual element;

– Contrary to popular opinion, it is no more wasteful in its targeting than many other tools (e.g. sales force, brochures, press releases, exhibitions).

Advertising – Weaknesses

– Generally, only direct response advertising works at the Conviction to Purchase stages;

– Advertising, unless it is direct response advertising, works by repetition over time. It becomes very expensive;

– The message should be clear and simple. It is not therefore a good tool for getting across detailed messages.

Public Relations
covers a range of activities, from media relations to dealing with shareholders, customers, government, the City, etc. To varying degrees these are essential areas for every organisation to address (see Chapter 7). As an optional tool we are really talking about media relations.

Media relations – Strengths

– Editorial coverage is good for shaping and confirming impressions, i.e. it works best at the Understanding and Favourable disposition levels;

– It has the semblance of third party, objective endorsement;

– It allows for a more developed explanation than, say, advertising;

– The cost is not usually seen at the time.

Media relations – Weaknesses

– There is no guarantee the release or article will appear;

– What does appear is not controllable and any promotion will tend to be only a small part of the article;

– Coverage could even be hostile;

– PR people, whether external agency or in-house staff, tend to be expensive.

Sponsorship – Strengths

– Can be used at different stages of the buying process, e.g. as an alternative to Advertising to spread awareness, e.g. Cornhill and cricket; or as an entertainment forum for existing clients to stiffen conviction;

– Can bring a welcome association with third-party activity e.g. charitable, Arts, sport, popular personality (see Case Study 6: Jones Lang Wootton);

– Can be used when other tools are not welcome or allowed, e.g. in schools, or to promote tobacco;

– Can be very cost-effective.

Sponsorship – Weaknesses

- High profile activities are very expensive – not just in terms of sponsorship fees, but the extra activities involved in taking full advantage;
- The sponsorship is secondary to the activity;
- Co- or junior sponsorship can go largely unnoticed;
- The brand may become known, but not the service it offers;
- Individual sponsorship is risky – personalities can fall from grace;
- Often not easy to measure the benefit.

Brochures – Strengths

- Enable full explanation and therefore good at the Understanding and Favourable disposition levels;
- Totally controllable;
- Useful in harness with other tools, e.g. sales force, exhibitions, mailings;
- Comparatively low cost.

Brochures – Weakness

- Reader knows it is promotional text and filters accordingly;
- Tend to be used over time and so can become dated.

Direct marketing – Strengths

- Can be targeted individually;
- Usable from Understanding to Conviction stages;
- Comparatively low cost;
- Useful in harness with other tools, e.g. telemarketing with sales force.

Direct marketing – Weakness

– Typically low responses mean high wastage rates.

Seminars & conferences – Strengths

Can be targeted individually;

– Usable from Understanding to Conviction stages;

– Enable mixing of targets with existing clients, for third-party endorsement;

– Comparatively low cost.

Seminars & conferences – Weaknesses

– Take a lot of preparation to work well;

– Rely on presentation skills.

Exhibitions – Strengths

– Can work at all stages from Awareness (stand) *see illustrations on page 78-9* to Purchase (sales force);

– Allows intensive market contact in short period;

– Projection is controllable.

Exhibitions – Weaknesses

– Audience is not guaranteed;

– Requires considerable preparation by marketing staff and sales force;

– Can be expensive.

Promotional items – Strengths

–   Useful in maintaining relationships at the Conviction stage
    of buying;

–   Wide choice of gifts available enables selection appropriate
    to target.

Promotional items – Weakness

–   Tend to be distributed indiscriminately, leading to high
    wastage.

Given the prominent use of sales forces in the property sector
it is at first sight surprising that sales force support has not been
fully developed in the sector. One reason is that many of the sales
forces do not see themselves as such. Most organisations also tend
not to be large – they do not have sales forces of several hundred
as in other industry sectors. The number of projects and
instructions being given is similarly limited. This makes life harder
for the marketing professional in that mounting a half decent
campaign in support of the sales force tends to cost several
thousand pounds. This is fine when there are hundreds of
instructions to be chased, but in a market where two instructions
= success, one = break-even, and none = failure, the enthusiasm
for mounting campaigns will inevitably be lessened.

What has received a lot of attention in recent years is
branding. Another result of organisations being smaller is that the
individuals in them become relatively more important. This is
very much the case in all professional services where the personal
relationship between client and firm is critical. We have already
seen the need to establish a personality for the firm as a means of
differentiation from the competition. In larger organisations the
brand will be a more corporate identity. In smaller organisations,
the firm's personality will in part be an amalgam of the collective
personalities of its leading partners or directors. This can be
supported and evidenced visually through branding.

Much has been written about the cost of branding, the most
striking example being the £10 million BP are supposed to have
spent worldwide on their recent exercise. The important thing to
recognise is that branding is not simply a coat of paint or a visual

device. Like any packaging, it must be consistent with its contents. The projection adopted therefore should reflect the culture and personality of the organisation.

Increasingly, as clients operate over a broader area geographically and demand a greater number of services, they will wish to be reassured that, wherever they are, they will receive the same, consistent quality of service. This can only be proven with experience, but an organisation should at least look as though it has its act together. Consistent representation visually of the brand will help achieve this. The issue of branding has become more significant in the sector in the 1990s and many organisations have addressed it in a professional way. (See Case Study 5: Knight Frank.)

The task of selecting the marketing tools to use then depends on the target audience, the communication need and the worth of the company of getting that communication across. We will develop further the selection of marketing tools, and how to use them effectively, in the next Chapter when we look at running the Marketing operation.

Reference

1. Cleaveley, E. (1983)
Marketing in the industrial and commercial property market, Estates Gazette.

2. Morgan, N.A. (1990)
Communications and the reality of marketing in professional service firms, International Journal of Advertising 9: 283 – 93.

Case study 4: Test marketing

This case study relates how a totally new service, Estates Gazette Interactive (EGi), was launched in the summer of 1996.

Background

By the spring of 1996, the Estates Gazette had prepared an interactive new service accessible on screen. The rationale for the development was that such facilities were becoming available, and the EG was determined to stay at the forefront of publishing within the sector by embracing this technology. A significant investment had already been made in this development, but more was required to launch the service. As Stewart Jones of EGi says: "Although we were confident in what we had developed, we felt it was critical that we got the service right at the launch stage."

With any conceptually new service it is difficult to predict market reaction. Quite the best way is to try the service in practice – in fact to test market the service. This is what EG decided to do.

The test

EG needed a mix of users to act as guinea pigs and supply feedback. The leading firms of surveyors were visited and the concept was explained. The firms were asked for their help in assessing the service. Nine firms agreed to try the service out through 21 individual users. This subsequently became12 firms and 30 individuals during the course of the test.

The test was scheduled to last two months, during which time the users would have installed as close as possible an arrangement to the real thing. No charges were applied in this period. Each firm had a total of four visits during the test period. The first was for the installation (and, where necessary, the provision of a loan modem). Each pilot user then had an introductory training session, followed by two feedback sessions, one at the end of the first week and the second about three weeks later.

The aim of the first feedback was to highlight any broad observations about the service and to identify any problems or difficulties. The sessions were conducted by an interviewer leading the discussion with a prompt sheet. The second feedback sessions were able to collect more constructive feedback based on the greater use of the service by that time. These were also conducted by an interviewer, using a structured questionnaire, both one-to-one and in groups.

The 30 users covered a range of disciplines: investment, office and retail agency, professional services, research, information services and so on. The issues covered included views on the services themselves, as well as the ease of using them.

Result

The test gave EGi a clear picture of the likely acceptance of the service and its usage. The likely popularity of the different service elements was also measured. Some specific suggestions were made as to improvements that would be welcome.

The feedback offered:

1. Fine tuning to the service so that the EG could launch EGi with confidence to the market at large;

2. The ability to predict what questions or misunderstandings about the service there might be in the market. EGi was able to address these issues quickly and smoothly.

3. Some suggested enhancements that might be introduced in the medium term.

This feedback justified the time and effort spent on the test marketing and contributed to the smooth launch and excellent take-up of EGi. By the end of October 1996, over 300 companies had signed up. As Stewart Jones says: "We did believe there would be a real demand for this service, and the pilot strengthened our conviction. We are, though, well pleased with the market reaction so far."

See illustrations on pages 72 and 148

Case study 5: Branding

Background

In mid-1994, Knight Frank & Rutley determined to adjust its branding. The firm had grown to more than 100 offices in 20 countries worldwide. This included a variety of local brand names, though all had Knight Frank in their title. KFR recognised that the increasingly international client base demanded a more consistent brand worldwide. There were no structural changes envisaged, but the firm was clear that its visual identity was integral to differentiating itself in the market.

The programme

It was decided to appoint an external design consultant to design the visual identity and to produce a detailed identity manual. A number of discussions were held throughout the firm to ensure that everyone was at one with the brief. The consultants selected were Sampson Tyrrell.

The internal discussions identified some broad, common goals: the existing name and logo were important but needed to be standardised; a balance had to be struck between modernity and keeping the firm's traditional values; the solution had to be applicable to both residential and commercial work; and it had to work worldwide. The audiences for whom the branding had to be acceptable were clients, potential clients, the industry at large, and staff.

The brief that was given to Sampson Tyrrell was specific:

1. Some name changes were required to achieve common branding worldwide. The names Knight Frank, however, were sacrosanct;

2. The new identity had to be instantly recognisable as belonging to the firm to ensure a seamless transition. For this reason, the traditional green and red colours and the symbol were to be maintained;

3. The personality of the firm had to be maintained. It was suggested that a serif typeface was therefore expected;

4. The solution had to work internationally and in both residential and commercial markets;

5. It had to have impact and be simple to interpret;

6. It had to be easily reproduced.

As Marketing Associate Sophie Rush says: "Essentially what the firm was looking for was an evolutionary rather than revolutionary branding that would project the firm worldwide as a single, co-ordinated entity."

All in all, the programme took 18 months as it went through the following stages of introduction:

1. Briefing / audit

2. Implementation planning

3. Options

4. Application

5. Development

6. Guidelines.

These stages were necessary given the wide range of environments in which the brand has to be effective: stationery; interior and exterior signage; advertising; brochures; property particulars; boards, banners and flags; presentational material; exhibition material; and promotional items. The exterior signage in the UK alone involved 29 different offices.

The launch of the new branding was timed for January 1, 1996 for impact and to coincide with the commencement of the firm's centenary year. A celebratory booklet, recalling events in Knight Frank & Rutley's history, and confirming the new branding, was prepared for distribution on this date to clients and throughout the sector.

The solution

The finally selected identity was presented to the partners who, in turn, briefed the staff. Perhaps the most significant step was the adoption of the single title "Knight Frank" worldwide. This meant dropping the "& Rutley" in Britain, "Hooker" in Australia and so on.

Otherwise, the identity fulfilled the aim of evolution rather than revolution. The revised name entailed a reconfiguration of the name and symbol (as below). The down strokes of the K and the F, with the symbol to the right, create a strong rectangular shape that works well on stationery and as a logo block on publicity material. It is equally strong when reversed out of dark backgrounds.

The firm's name is shown in a specially drawn typeface, created to retain the character of the former identity yet carry more impact. The spacing and cleaner lines of the letters ensure the impact and create a better legibility, which is needed for the small-scale environments in which the logo sometimes appears.

The corporate typefaces adopted were Stone Serif for use on all printed items and marketing material. This is a face readily available internationally. Computer-generated material uses Times typeface.

A full explanation of the corporate identity and its uses is set out in Knight Frank's Identity Guidelines. These offer clear working examples and "summarise how our identity can be used consistently and therefore effectively to protect a strong brand image".

The guidelines *(see illustration on page 72)* are an excellent example of how to implement and manage a corporate identity and they deservedly won the Special Judges' Award in the UK Property Marketing Awards 1995. The ready acceptance of the new identity, within the firm, the market and throughout the world is further testimony to the success of the programme.

Case study 6: Sponsorship

The aim

In 1990 Jones Lang Wootton celebrated the 25th anniversary of its opening in Brussels. To commemorate this the firm looked to organise an event to achieve a number of aims:

- to demonstrate JLW's serious position as part of the business community of Brussels
- to offer the opportunity to entertain clients
- public relations.

The solution

The activity Jones Lang Wootton selected was to sponsor the cleaning of the public statues in the Parc Royale, the principal park at the heart of Brussels between the royal palace and the parliament. The programme was launched at a press conference held jointly with the City authority who were organising the cleaning programme. The authority was naturally happy to encourage a private organisation in setting a good example of cultural support.

The programme of work took three months to complete, the only surprise being that, as foliage was cleared, the envisaged 38 statues became 52. To celebrate the completed task, Jones Lang Wootton threw a party in the park for 1,000 guests. Eight government ministers, members of the City authority, clients of the firm and media attended.

The result

The sponsorship achieved all of its aims. The project captured the public imagination and profiled the firm in a very positive way. Moreover, the fact that it was associated with physical structures gave the sponsorship a relevance for a property firm. Nor was the cost prohibitive – in fact, sponsoring the cleaning of the statues cost less than the party. *See illustration on page 76*

Michel Pilette, head of JLW in Brussels adds: "We were very pleased with the initiative which, I would say, represented good value for money as a promotion." Jones Lang Wootton have since capitalised on this positive association with support for culture with a continuing programme of sponsorship.

- the restoration of a major painting of Otto Venus in 1994 "Antwerp cultural"

- the restoration of the statue of St. Nepornuk in front of the parliament in Luxembourg

- and the current project, restoring the organ of the Notre Dame de Laeken church in Brussels, in association with the royal foundation and the churches of Belgium.

The programme represents an excellent example of the use of sponsorship as a promotional tool. It is wholly positive in profiling the firm seriously, it has a public appeal, it offers attractive opportunities to entertain clients and it is affordable.

Case study 7: Advertising

Background

How does a firm of property consultants raise its "brand awareness"? This was the issue facing Nelson Bakewell a few years ago. The conventional route for advisers has been to promote themselves by association. By associating their firms with the activities of their client base – deals, developments, etc. – they can project a statement about the quality of the services they provide. Firms that have been established for many years can also stress their solidity and longevity. Despite the fact that former glories are no guarantee of present success, many clients will be rightly attracted to a firm that has a proven track record and has flourished in the property business over several decades.

Beyond these routes, the opportunities for what can be called "corporate advertising" – or raising brand awareness – have been limited. Corporate advertisements in the property trade press are seen by a readership which mostly comprises not the target client market but the competition – other firms of property consultants. While advertising in publications such as the Financial Times would undoubtedly reach the right target market, the cost of doing so makes an extended campaign extremely costly.

By 1988, Nelson Bakewell was well aware of these dilemmas. The chartered surveying firm had been established six years previously by Phillip Nelson and Simon Bakewell. It had grown quickly and successfully: staff numbered over 100, its client list included established Landlord and Tenant names, and it was involved in high profile developments ranging from Berkeley Square to the Midlands. The time was right for the firm to embark on its next phase of business development and that required raising its profile in the market-place and broadening its client base. As a young, successful and innovative firm it had a message to put across but it was not prepared to wait for the "drip-feed" of promotion by association, and could not play the "tradition" card by pointing to decades of experience in the business.

The campaign

At the same time as Nelson Bakewell was pondering its options on improving its "brand awareness", two events in the broadcasting industry were laying the ground for the first major sponsorship deal between a radio station and a firm of property consultants. Prior to this point in time, broadcasting legislation prevented sponsorship of news and current affairs programming on commercial radio. However, a new Broadcasting Bill and deregulation ushered in a more relaxed regime which was intended to open up broadcasting for greater competition and introduce new forms of funding. This new competition in the radio business was reflected by the take-over of the long-established London radio station, LBC by the media conglomerate, Crown.

The new station – LBC Crown FM – aimed itself at the business community and so was a good match for Nelson Bakewell. In 1989, when the firm agreed to sponsor the daily two-hour "drive time" business programme, LBC sponsorship executive Bob Cole commented on the ground breaking nature of the deal: "Nelson Bakewell is a real breakthrough in two ways. It introduces sponsorship to a news-based programme in a perfectly legitimate way and it is the first campaign to be aimed at a specific target audience. Until now, our sponsors have been mass-market orientated."

It was this focused opportunity that attracted Nelson Bakewell. In the past, other firms of chartered surveyors had dabbled with advertising on both television and general radio programming but had little response because of the hugely diffuse nature of the audience.

The structure of the initial Nelson Bakewell/LBC sponsorship was that the sponsors would get regular namechecks throughout the two-hour programme and also devise a series of adverts to run during the segment. The first challenge was to devise a catchline that would accompany the namechecks; it would be ineffective if all the listeners heard was the name without any reference to what Nelson Bakewell actually did!

Given this brief, the firm's advertising agency came up with: "*Nelson Bakewell Chartered Surveyors. Traditional Service in the Modern Manner*". It was to be a slogan that served the firm very well. It stated what they were and conveyed what they offered: a traditional (high quality/reliable) standard of service blended with the innovation and speed of the contemporary business world. With the catchline established, the next task was to explain exactly what Nelson Bakewell as "chartered surveyors" could do for the listening audience.

Over the first two years of sponsorship, the style of the adverts was refined and diversified. Some were broadly factual to coincide with significant events in the property calendar (rating revaluations, etc.), some featured Nelson Bakewell directors highlighting particular areas of interest for property owners/occupiers and some employed humour to get the message across. By 1992, the actor and writer, Stephen Fry had been recruited to perform the commercials. The following is a typical example of the kind of material which was used to get the Nelson Bakewell message across:

Stephen Fry: Did you know that you can actually improve the handling of your commercial property interests while making a cheese soufflé? Here's how?

Vigorous beating of egg whisk in bowl

Stephen Fry: Beat the whites of four fresh eggs until they're good and stiff. Meanwhile, make a quick call... Here's one I made earlier.

Push button dialling as Stephen mumbles
0171 629 6501

NB Receptionist: Good morning, Nelson Bakewell.

Stephen Fry: *Still whisking* There you are, it's as easy as that. Now back to the soufflé. Blend the cream with the egg yolks...*fades out*

NB Receptionist: Nelson Bakewell Chartered Surveyors. Traditional recipes – *cough* – **service** in the modern manner.

The series also used humour to tackle one of the perennial difficulties of radio advertising: getting people to remember the advertiser's telephone number. One advert featured Fry – supposedly taking a course in memory enhancement – just repeating the Nelson Bakewell telephone number with the punchline – "We do names next week" – followed closely by the namecheck. This approach helped the firm's image get away from the prevalent conceptions of the industry which had it peopled either by "gents in pinstripes" or "cowboys". It portrayed a firm that was on-the-ball, alert to the needs of its clients but not too stuffy.

Results

If the format is successful in generating listener response and awareness, the next most important step is to institute a system which can measure those factors and turn the interest into business. One specific campaign within the sponsorship which was designed to alert occupiers to a forthcoming rating revaluation generated several hundred calls. Dealing with and tracking those inquiries was a major operation for Nelson Bakewell. Additional resources had to be put into the switchboard and special "Feedback Forms" were developed so that staff could register work or business leads that were flowing from the radio. Perhaps surprisingly, there were relatively few "time wasting" leads. Although the types of businesses contacting Nelson Bakewell ranged, literally, from the biggest to the smallest, a very significant proportion of contacts led either directly to work or to "nursery" instructions which would lead to work in the future. Several clients were attracted by the notion of "growing together" with an emergent firm, and some saw the Nelson Bakewell campaign as bringing some much-needed straightforwardness to the property consultancy business. The following is typical of comments being received from the new client base generated by the radio:

"In response to your advertising, and having heard the horror stories of the cowboys operating in this field, I rather tentatively enquired of your office if they felt they might be able to do something about our extortionate rates bill. I am happy to report that had I been the chairman of ICI, I could not have been treated more helpfully and courteously".

When the sponsorship had been running for several months, Nelson Bakewell began to register another benefit aside from these concrete business leads. Surveyors began to find that when pitching in competitive situations against other firms – often firms with more established pedigrees – the potential clients "knew" the Nelson Bakewell brand when previously that would not have been the case. The radio was beginning to produce a brand awareness which gave the firm an invaluable platform from which to capture new business. Consequently, the firm's ratio of instructions secured to pitches given began to improve steadily.

At the outset, the sponsorship was a considerable financial commitment. To put the cost in perspective, in the first year the outlay was equivalent to taking the front page corporate advertisement in the leading property trade magazine every week. However, what was vividly demonstrated over the five years of sponsorship was the importance of "making a splash" early on. Radio – like television – should not be approached as a "toe-in-the-water" proposition. If approached tentatively it is more than likely that the brand message will not have time to register. One-off short campaigns may be appropriate for marketing a particular building or service but they are unlikely to raise the brand awareness of a firm.

Because Nelson Bakewell plunged into the medium so forcefully it had the effect of not only immediately raising this awareness but it also meant that the firm became the talk of the industry – the knock-on promotion was considerable. This enabled the firm to reduce its commitment and financial exposure to the sponsorship as time went on. When the sponsorship concluded in 1994, the annual cost was running at 30% of the 1989 level and was focused on a specific "commercial property slot" which ran within the business programme. Because of Nelson Bakewell's long-term commitment to the station, LBC had developed this editorial segment to give a focus for the NB advertising. The slot became very much part of the property business' media scene and, as such, produced spin-off benefits for both Nelson Bakewell and LBC.

During this latter period, the results of the campaign were still very tangible. This feedback from one of the firm's divisional directors was typical of the kind of business that was still flowing from the sponsorship:

New client contact which resulted directly from the radio sponsorship has led to the sale of a site in the Earls Court Road (c.£9,000 fee) and a subsequent instruction on around £3m-worth of further property.

This was also the time when the radio exposure led to Nelson Bakewell securing one of its largest corporate clients – a large North-American computer company which is still a major client of the firm and generating business some three years later.

Viewed as a whole, what this demonstrates is the snowball effect of a long-term relationship with a particular medium: as a campaign continues, awareness grows at a disproportionate rate. Indeed at the time of writing, many people in the property industry still think that Nelson Bakewell advertise on the radio despite the fact that it is over two years since the firm has done so. Although the end of the relationship in 1994 was triggered finally by a change in the ownership and direction of LBC, the sponsorship had already been judged by Nelson Bakewell as having come to the end of its natural life. Research within the industry showed a rate of awareness of the Nelson Bakewell name and the sponsorship of nearly 70%.

Conclusions

At the conclusion of the campaign, several facts about using radio to increase the brand awareness of a service provider had been demonstrated. First, it highlighted the necessity to make a big entrance into the medium: otherwise effectiveness and money will be dissipated.

Once it has been established that the target audience is appropriate, it is vital to tailor content to that audience. The listeners to a London-wide radio station are not the same as the readers of a property trade journal: what you are offering as a service-provider has to be demystified and presented in terms of what it can do for the consumer. As discussed above, it is important to combine content with humour and ingenuity; if the listener is not engaged they will not be impelled to contact the advertiser.

Finally, and perhaps most significantly, the sponsorship campaign – like any successful marketing initiative – showed the importance of being first! The very originality of what Nelson Bakewell did as a firm of chartered surveyors generated a huge amount of publicity and new business. Although the campaign cannot be said to have precluded other firms from following the lead, it did mean that for five years Nelson Bakewell more or less had the medium to itself.

Ali Ballantine
Marketing Associate
NELSON BAKEWELL

Chapter 7

Controlling marketing

Most organisations in the commercial property sector have moved on from appointing a marketing partner, perhaps with some external agency support, to look after marketing issues. Many are making a significant investment in marketing: both in terms of the employment of staff and external agencies; and in terms of marketing expenditure.

Consistent with the scale of the investment is the need to direct and control the marketing effort to ensure the investment is well made. Few would argue with this, though the way that direction and control is applied still varies considerably.

In the worst cases the management of the company will decide the level of the marketing budget according to what it feels it can afford. The amount will probably relate to the previous year's figure and be a vote of x% up or down on that figure. The marketing department may or may not have submitted a request for budget in advance of this. Typically, too, the department may be told which activities the management 'favours' and which are to be cut back or eliminated. This process of course totally misses the point and such a company will not get the best out of its investment in what it chooses to call marketing.

In better run companies the marketing function plays an active role in the business planning round. There is every reason why this should be the case and they relate to what marketing is. We have seen in Chapter 2 that marketing entails Finding out about the market, the company and the company's position within the market. The business plan is where the agreed assessment of the company's position should be stated and the key targets set for future business development.

Similarly, any Adapting that is required within the company, as a response to perceived market needs, should also be set out in the business plan. And, finally, the communication programmes required to deliver the agreed targets need to be identified.

The marketing department of any organisation is in a uniquely favoured position to perform this role. This department alone has been voted the time to monitor the performance of the company in its market. The department is in a sense a window on the outside world, reflecting views both inwards and outwards.

Where a company is not using a marketing function in the business planning process, it may be as much a lack of development in its strategic planning processes as in its understanding of marketing.

Strategic planning

Every company has a different approach towards business planning and there is no single fixed formula to be adopted. The process should, though, allow the company to review its present position; determine where it intends to go; set out how to get there; and how to monitor performance. Each company may give its plan a different title but, typically, what will be produced is a strategic plan, presenting a medium-/long- term view and reviewable annually; and a budget, a one-year control document with detailed financial forecasts.

The planning process may take several months and should continue a "top down" and "bottom up" dialogue between senior management and operating units. A typical process might be:

Strategic planning – a typical process

1. **Corporate appraisal**
    The current position and discernible trends, reviewed against the business environment.

2. **Mission statement**
    The long-term purpose and direction.

3. **Goal statements**
    Statements of broad future aspirations in specific areas.

4. **Objective statements**
    Setting key results that deliver the goal statements.

5. **Strategic initiatives**
    Descriptions of how key results are to be achieved.

6. **Financial projections**
    Quantification of the plan content.

1.   Corporate appraisal

This analysis is a review by management of the company's current position and the forces that are expected to impact on its markets. There are a number of techniques that management can use to arrive at a common understanding both of the business and its markets, such as SWOT analysis, Comparative Business Analysis and Critical Success Factors.

A SWOT analysis is an assessment of a company's Strengths and Weaknesses and the Opportunities and Threats facing it. Strengths and Weaknesses are assessed in competitive terms and should be internal factors within the control of management. Opportunities are areas for likely profit performance and Threats are external forces imposing pressure or constraint.

By Comparative Business Analysis, management assesses the prospects for the sectors the company is in, and the company's competitive abilities in each. By identifying the key criteria for prospects and for capabilities and measuring the one against the other, a simple overview of the company's position in each sector can be obtained.

The Critical Success Factors technique involves, quite simply, identifying the key factors that determine business performance. With all these techniques, once management has arrived at a common understanding it can begin to formulate strategy. .

2.   Mission statement

The mission statement defines the long-term purpose and direction of the business. As such it should be sufficiently broad and lasting.

3.   Goal statements

These are broad statements of future aspirations in specific areas. They should set down the areas for which adequate resources will have to be made and should remain valid over the medium-term. Likely areas for goal statements to cover might be: markets; services; staff; IT; financial performance.

4.   Objective statements

Objective statements are formulated from the goal statements by focusing on a single key result to be aimed for. Each objective should be quantifiable and subsequently measurable, with a targeted date for achievement. As objectives are achieved they should be replaced with a fresh objective.

5.   Strategic initiatives

The strategic initiatives describe how each of the key results identified in stage 4. is to be achieved. These provide a framework within which specific action plans and responsibilities can be defined in more detail. Again they should be continually reviewed and updated against performance.

6.   Financial projections

These indicate the likely outcome of adopting the proposed strategies in financial terms. The sensitivity of the projections to any changes in market or economic assumptions should be included. The projections should adopt performance measurements that can be tracked by management at regular intervals.

The budget

Once the strategic plan is complete, the strategic direction will be available for constructing the budget which, usually, is a one year control document only.

The marketing department should have had an active involvement since stage 3, the goal statements. In stage 5 in particular, the description of how each Strategic Initiative is to be achieved will cover who is responsible for performances and what marketing activities will be required to help deliver them.

The marketing input to the budget round will therefore embrace each strategic initiative and cost the activities required within the budget period. The total marketing budget requested therefore will be the summation of the expenses needed to deliver the agreed business aims. This has the merit of containing expenditure to what is needed and not simply doing it because it was done last year. Contrary to popular belief, most marketing professionals do not seek to spend large sums for the sake of it, and would much prefer to cost expenditure carefully within the confines of the strategic planning process.

Adopting this process brings a greater realism to the use of marketing. If management finds the budget identified by Marketing to be excessive, it has two responses: either that the operating units can meet target with less support in terms of marketing activity; or to reduce the number of business objectives. The former may be a correct assessment, in which case results will confirm this within months, but it may also be self-delusion. This seriously risks undermining the credibility of the agreed strategic plan. The latter, therefore, is usually the sensible option, particularly as there is a natural tendency to set too many objectives in the first place.

Assessing the marketing budget

Once the marketing department has the agreed objective statements, it is in a position to put together the programme of marketing activities. This will be a relatively straightforward process given the department's involvement in assessing the company's market positioning. It will have the key information outlined in Chapter 6 for determining the combination of marketing tools to use: the targets to be approached; the communication tasks to be accomplished; the perceived value of that communication. The department will then assemble programmes for each strategic initiative drawing on its knowledge of media audiences; the effective role each tool can play, and costs.

We referred in the last chapter to different "buyers" being at different stages of the buying decision process and that, at any one time, a company has client contacts who are very loyal, warm, or merely cold prospects. This is a fundamental consideration in the strategic planning process.

The 80 : 20 rule applies for probably most companies in the property sector – that is 80% of fee income comes from only 20% of the clients. Indeed, I suspect that there are many who would happily settle for so "broad" a distribution of business.

There are several reasons why repeat business from an existing client is attractive: there is a limited cost entailed in acquiring the business; the working process is already established between you and should be quicker; and there is a greater certainty of payment. The down sides are that the client, knowing his own importance to you, may be very demanding; and fee margins may be reduced. All in all though, companies find existing clients attractive and seek to hold on to them.

It is not difficult to see that the need for marketing activities to convert someone from merely Understanding what you have to offer will be quite different from those required to convert someone who is already convinced, into purchasing more from you. The generation of repeat business, or cross-selling of other services, will depend very much on the personal relationship established. For this reason, many organisations have instituted an account handler system.

The basic premise of account handling is that one person is dedicated to ensuring his or her particular client is supplied with the best level of service possible. This is not just a quality control job. It entails developing a close understanding of the client's business aims so as to be better able to anticipate service needs and perform beyond the client's expectations. Temperamentally, this "nurturing" role calls for different personal skills from those of a business winner or "hunter". Support for the account handlers should be one of the key tasks for the marketing team.

If we refer to the tools listed in the previous chapter and their strengths and weaknesses, we can see that the tools appropriate to maintaining clients at the Conviction level in the buying process are such as: mailing, seminars, exhibitions, promotional items and, of course, the sales force who are the account handlers. This is a very different mix of activities from those that are appropriate for converting colder prospects.

With colder prospects we need to look at the tools that are good at generating Awareness, and building Understanding and Favourable disposition. These are advertising, sponsorship, exhibitions, brochures, media relations and telemarketing, all of which build a platform to help the sales force to be more effective.

This is not to suggest that each tool performs only these roles. Advertising and editorial comment, for instance, have a positive, reassuring impact on existing clients and staff as well as the unconvinced. It is just that they would be expensive tools for addressing these groups only.

The end result of this process will be that the marketing programme for the year ahead, and the resources – staff, agencies and activities – required to deliver it will be identified. The process is one of building the different elements to match the aims of the strategic plan. It is therefore a bottom-up response. This is why setting an overall figure based on previous expenditure misses the point. The marketing department cannot know what budget it is likely to need until the business planning process is concluded.

Getting the best out of the marketing department

We have seen that marketing embraces a wide range of activities. At one end of the scale there are the very mechanical, scientific tasks of research and analysing the market and the company's performance; at the other end there are the more creative, artistic activities of design and promotion. One of the appeals of working in marketing is that it does span such a range of mental processes. Equally there are many who develop their skills to a greater depth within the various marketing specialisms. Just like any other profession, the best job tends to be done when the appropriate specialist skills are applied.

In the same way that it is unlikely that an advertising copywriter would make a very good valuer of property, it is not reasonable to expect a property professional to be able to write a good advertisement. For some reason, however, some have tried – with embarrassing results. The moral is: use a professional. By the same token, like any good professional, marketing people will work more effectively if they acquire an understanding of property. This is particularly the case if they are producing written material, be it brochures, press releases or editorial. The standard marketing thought processes, however, should enable a good marketing professional from a different sector to be effective quickly.

The need to use specialist marketing help may entail employing external agencies: research, design, advertising, PR, conference organisers, direct marketing and so on. The younger and less established marketing is within the organisation the more likely it is that external help will be needed. As the business planning and marketing effort becomes more integrated and consistent, so the resources that are likely to be required over the medium term become discernable. Often then there is benefit in bringing a resource in-house, though you need to be very confident it will be fully utilised and that the investment will be worthwhile. Broadly, the advantages of using in-house and agency marketing resources are as follows:

In-house advantages

Known quality of performance
Performance more controllable
Speed of response
Usually saves money
Gets to know the organisation better

Agency advantages

Brings fresh thinking
External and objective
Can offer more developed skills
May be accorded more credibility by management
Only incurs cost as used

Most organisations, even where marketing is well developed and practised, use a combination of in-house marketing staff and external agencies. This should ensure the highest level of performance and the best investment of resource. What is to be recommended is that external agencies are selected, briefed and managed by the in-house professionals. There are three fundamental reasons for this: professionalism, briefing and cost control.

In all walks of life the adage that "it takes one to know one" holds. Patently, if professional skills are sought, then those with the most experience in that profession will be best placed to identify quality. The in-house marketing staff should therefore be involved in short-listing and selecting external agencies. For the same fundamental reason, briefing the agency in terms that are likely to encourage the best response, and managing performance within budget should be the remit of the in-house professional.

This is an area that has improved significantly in the property sector. A few years ago below-standard work or excessive fees were being claimed as a result of agencies being employed by property professionals who did not have experience in marketing. Like any other sector, marketing agencies have seen their margins shrink in recent years and seemingly some, on occasion, took the opportunity to increase their margins when they felt they could get away with it, either by raising the price or by applying less effort to the job. By and large now, the quality of work carried out is of a very high order. Like their property counterparts, UK marketing agencies are probably the finest in the world when briefed and managed properly.

Whether in-house or external, motivating marketing people is very rarely a problem. Their whole training is to seek to change things for the better. They are by nature, therefore, optimists and, being closely involved in communicating the organisation's strengths to the market, tend to become passionately committed to the cause. This enthusiasm will always be best generated and directed, though, when the briefing is thorough and they are made to feel part of the team.

The importance of a good brief cannot be over-emphasised. Not only should it set out clearly what is expected, but it should also set out the rationale for the job. By definition the result can never be better than the brief, so it is worth taking the time and trouble to explain the background to the task. This will enable the marketing professional to think about your problem more constructively and, probably, come up with a better solution.

The best agencies will always ask questions about the brief to arrive at this better understanding. One marketing consultant I know sometimes, and tactfully, suggests to the client that the brief needs amending. This is brave, and occasionally to his short-term cost, but the end result for those clients mature enough to listen is a more effective job. Adopting a "need to know" only attitude to briefing will guarantee under-performance, and erring on the side of too much information usually pays off.

A by-product of inadequate briefing is wrangling over delivery times or invoices. Again a fellow marketing professional will be best placed to agree with an agency precisely what processes are to be employed, the time entailed, and what is reasonable cost.

It follows that, if we expect a professional to perform for us, we have to trust them to a certain extent in the execution of their skills. Be open-minded therefore when the marketing agency or staff come back with proposals, though certainly expect them to have a rationale to justify their proposals. They are, after all, coming at the task as an outsider which may be more relevant.

This does not mean to suggest that every proposal should be accepted. Having employed an "enfant terrible" of the UK advertising world in my last job, I had to turn down some high impact creative work simply because the imagery he was proposing represented too uncomfortable an association of ideas for my employer. It would have been, however, bold and powerful advertising and I appreciated having my parameters challenged. As far as possible, give creative people their head and don't impose your subjective tastes upon them. The risk if you do is that their enthusiasm will wane and, if it is an agency, you'll end up being served by the third team and get dull work.

There are two further recommendations I would make in regard to using agencies. The first is that I would be wary of using agencies for a range of different marketing activities. Even the biggest PR or advertising agencies have their core specialisms and, while they may claim a much broader range of competence, you will probably be better advised to pick horses for courses.

The second recommendation I would make is to avoid remuneration on a time spent basis. The basic selection of the communication initiative is made partly on the assessment of the value of that initiative. Given that the worth of the communication is known, then the value of using the agency is also known and they must be briefed to work within this. The open-ended nature of time spent remuneration does not easily sit with this. It also expends energy on monitoring and checking and almost inevitably, even between professionals, "how did this task take so long?" type discussions, from which there are no winners. Whether the agency's task is a single project or on-going their performance should be judged on effectiveness of output not time sheets.

All of the foregoing relates to the appointment of marketing professionals on the basis of their professional skills. The examples of the restaurant in Chapter 3 and the property industry in Chapter 5 showed that the professional skill is only the core of the service offered. As with the other examples, the core advertising, PR, design or other skills might be the dominant factor in determining choice of supplier or staff. But these skills are not so scarce that we do not have a choice. Selection from short-list therefore tends to be made more on other service aspects, of which, probably, "ability to understand our particular needs" and personal empathy are probably the most important. This is especially the case when employing in-house marketing staff.

Measuring marketing performance

The investment in marketing, staff and expenditure, can be sizeable, so it makes sound commercial sense to measure the performance of that investment. Marketing staff should be leading the way in calling for such measurement, because monitoring the reaction to activities, and thereby reverting to the Finding out process, is the best way lessons can be learned and improvements generated. To see ways of assessing performance it is necessary to revisit the Finding out activities listed in Chapter 4.

It is important that, when monitoring and assessing, we remember to judge activities on the basis that they were selected in the first place. We should not therefore expect advertising, unless it is a direct response campaign, to deliver volumes of new business on its own. What we might reasonably expect, though, is increased levels of Awareness in the target market, or a higher success rate for the sales force in winning appointments as a result of the better market Understanding or more Favourable disposition. With advertising, it would be appropriate to arrange a research tracking study periodically, to assess awareness and attitude levels in the target market and to monitor the success rate in gaining appointments.

It would be fair to apply the ultimate test of sales figures to sales force performance assessment or to campaigns combining a range of tools, including the sales force. It may occasionally be appropriate to assess advertising or direct marketing in this way. At Lloyds Bowmaker some years ago I ran a multi-million pound advertising campaign, the success of which rested on acquiring direct response lending business. The only way these particular loans came was through this advertising and, provided the advertising costs amounted to within a certain percentage of the total volumes of lending, the advertising was judged successful. This, though, was a specific case and not one that readily transfers to the property area.

The other principal areas for Finding out, listed in Chapter 4, were media comment, client feedback and research. Publications can help measure performance in two ways. Specifically, monitoring media coverage will help to assess the performance of the PR team, while industry comment generally will convey how effective the overall communication effort is working. This may not be precisely measurable but over time it will provide a picture.

Client feedback is very useful on two counts: firstly, and obviously, because it is very important and secondly, because it may often cover activities the effects of which are difficult to measure otherwise, such as: brochures, seminars and conferences, promotional items, sales force performance. Client feedback also, of course, is qualitative rather than quantitative. The one flaw with client feedback is that the response is "a sample of one" which may be subjective and unreliable. Client feedback can be collective in research or through industry awards.

The most meaningful industry awards are where entrants are obliged to explain their initiative and provide evidence of its success. Within the property sector there are such awards now and indeed a number of winners of The Company of Chartered Surveyors' UK Property Marketing Awards are included in this book as case studies.

Formal research studies, next to sales figures, probably tell a company more about its marketing performance than any other forms of feedback. Their great strengths are that they are objective, can concentrate on whatever issues the company wishes to measure, can be quantitative and qualitative and, importantly, they are confidential.

All of these measurement processes assess the effectiveness of marketing communications as they impact on the market. What is tougher to assess is the organisation's overall approach to marketing. There are, however, now available benchmarking studies which enable organisations to measure how their own approach compares with other British companies.

The Marketing Council is currently encouraging companies to benchmark their performance and has developed a set of comparisons within the service sector. The approach is essentially one of self-assessment of behaviour on a number of pre-selected issues. This self-assessment may then be submitted for independent external analysis, in confidence, and comparative performance fed back. The value is probably not so much in seeing the comparative assessment, but in going through the issues together internally. The aim of The Marketing Council in promoting this is to encourage management to go through the very issues that are consistent with being client-led and giving marketing proper attention.

It is not difficult to control marketing performance and to guarantee its effectiveness. What is required is for management to embrace marketing in its strategic planning, to employ competent marketing professionals, whether in-house or externally, and to vote and manage the resources identified from the strategic planning process as necessary to delivering the business aims.

Section **Two**

Property marketing

This section looks specifically at the concept and practice of marketing property. Chapter 8 asks whether "marketing" is the correct term to apply, covers those marketing activities that are relevant, and looks at some of the more recent developments that are changing the nature of property marketing.

Chapter 9 is devoted entirely to case studies, some of them award winners that demonstrate the high levels of thinking, preparation and execution that are now being successfully applied in the commercial property market.

Research into market requirements is vital to establish targets required & gives an insight into what prospective occupiers aspirations for the property is

Chapter 8

Is it really marketing?

'Within commercial property the term "marketing" is most commonly used with reference to the disposal of property. Yet there has to be some doubt as to whether the term "marketing" is correctly applied when we are talking of property disposal.

When a landlord instructs an agent to dispose of his property or to let vacant space, does the agent truly practise marketing? Let us apply the test of our defined marketing process: Find out, Adapt, Communicate.

In the case of a new development, provided that the agent is brought on board at a sufficiently early stage, then it is clear that a marketing role truly is performed. Sometimes, and increasingly since the overcapacity generated at the end of the 1980s, specific research is carried out as to market requirements before development goes ahead. In any case, agents are well informed as to market requirements as a result of their own market knowledge and also the weight of formal research carried out now by most competent surveying firms. This does enable them to target prospective occupiers more carefully and to understand what it is those targets require. This initial finding out stage can also entail the agents exploring and sourcing the institutional or other funding prepared to back the development. While more research might be undertaken, particularly for large developments, it is probably fair to claim that a Finding out process of sorts is adopted in most development cases.

Where the biggest question mark arises is at the Adapting stage. It is true that, with new or re-developments, a genuine product shaping role is performed. I have sat in meetings with developers and architects and, for both retail and office projects, seen the product reshaped to fit perceived tenant and user requirements. Change of use also is increasingly being considered for re-developments. The product is therefore genuinely Adapted.

For an existing property, however, the scope for Adaption will be very limited. The basic product exists, in its location, and of its type. I acknowledge that certain product improvements can be effected: the space might be reconfigured, offered in phases, refurbished, the pricing adjusted and so on, provided the landlord is prepared to accept the advice. Too often, though, agents are reduced in their product shaping to selecting favourable features of the property and matching them to what appeals to the market. On the Adapting test, therefore, much property marketing can be seen to be not truly marketing.

As far as the third leg of the marketing process is concerned, Communicating, then patently this is practised vigorously. Many use the word marketing when they really mean communicating, promoting, offering or selling.

All in all then it is fair to say that property marketing contains a number of elements and practices of marketing, but where the ability to change the product is not present then it would be incorrect to call it marketing. It follows that where the finding out and adapting processes of marketing are not practised, there is the greatest risk of an empty building.

Much as agents might like to be involved only in proper marketing exercises, the reality is that they frequently have to make the best of it. Even where there is no scope to reshape the product, it is still beneficial to think marketing. This helps to identify the targets and those product features that will appeal to them. Equally important is the identification of the negative features so that these can be countered as far as possible.

The selection of promotional tools will also depend on the identification of the level potential clients are at in the buying process. Is the main hurdle to overcome that of awareness, of understanding, disposition, conviction or final selection? In practical terms will the greatest difficulty be in communicating the offer, getting them to view, bring colleagues to view, like it when they do view, to agree terms or what? An assessment of where the key communication hurdles lie will help define which promotional activities should be selected and where the weight of effort should be expended.

Developments in property marketing

The competitive nature of the market has given rise to many improvements in property marketing in recent years. Here are just some of the advancements made:

1. Use of research

Lessons do seem to have been learned from the market downturn. Increasingly, both developers and occupiers are commissioning research studies before proceeding with projects or moving into markets. This is particularly the case with international projects where inevitably the scale of investment and lower familiarity with the market renders the project potentially riskier. Colin Hargreaves, head of Healey & Baker's City team, recalls that "the developers of Broadgate must have spent nearly two years speaking to potential occupiers to define their needs".

The use of research extends also to the selling process. Developers who have commissioned research into the catchment potential for their scheme have in their hands precisely the very reassurance that would-be occupiers seek before committing to a scheme. Research demonstrating market potential has become an integral part of the selling kit, particularly on major international projects when cross-border tenants are sought.

This reflects the level that potential tenants are at in the buying process. For example, the scheme will vary as a concept for the targeted tenants depending on where they are from. When I prepared the marketing plan for a retail scheme on Kirchberg plateau, just outside Luxembourg city a few years ago, we judged that the product to be sold varied according to the target audience.

Target location	Product
Local	The scheme
National	Kirchberg + the scheme
International	Luxembourg + Kirchberg + the scheme

In other words, all a local retailer needed to be sold was the scheme because he already knew the market. The international retailer, however, needed to be convinced that Luxembourg represented a viable market, that Kirchberg was a good location within it, and that the scheme would offer a good base from which to trade. The promotional material we prepared reflected these needs.

Promoting the location as well as the building has always been a well recognised need within the sector. This though has intensified in recent years as towns, regions and countries have all appreciated that they are in competition with one another for inward investment. As a result, most towns of any size now actively promote themselves and produce a range of economic and demographic data to support their case. As Kotler, Haider and Rein say in their book Marketing Places: "Places that fail to market themselves successfully face the risk of economic stagnation and decline."[1]. The vigorous competition for the right to hold international events shows that this is well appreciated. The benefits accruing from staging the Olympic Games to such recent winners as Barcelona (1992) and Atlanta (1996) demonstrate why.

The publication of research studies measuring the relative attractiveness of leading cities emphasises the competitive nature of the market. On a national level, Black Horse Agencies produce an annual UK Relocation study in which UK companies nominate their favoured city for relocation. London won in 1996 and Birmingham and Bristol in previous years. Internationally, Healey & Baker's annual European Cities Monitor tracks European businessmen's attitudes towards the top 30 business cities. London has come top every year since 1990. The factors businessmen say are the most important in determining where to locate are demonstrated by their answers to the question in the survey (shown opposite).

It is clear that choice of location, for most, is a hard-headed business decision with market and communication factors dominating, cost factors secondary, and quality of life least important of all. Cities need to appreciate their own strengths and weaknesses in each of the critical factors. More specifically, they need to know how they are perceived so that they can correct any misperceptions. As an example, four years ago in the study Glasgow was rated only the 21st city in Europe for its international transport links in spite of considerable efforts to upgrade its airport. Since then Glasgow has promoted its air links and has steadily risen to 18th, 14th and 11th best city for international links in subsequent years.

A similarly negative perception was being promoted about new London locations in the Docklands and at Broadgate a few years ago by taxi drivers. It was recognised that cab drivers, by not

---

Essential factors for locating business

Q. I'd like to discuss some of the factors companies may consider
    when deciding where to locate their business. How important
    to your company is (each factor)?
    *Communication issues continue to dominate corporate
    thinking, followed by cost factors.*

	1996 % (base 509)	1995 %
Easy access to markets, customers or clients	63	66
Transport links with other cities and internationally	52	51
The quality of telecommunications	46	49
Cost and availability of staff	43	49
The climate governments create for business through tax polices and availability of financial incentives	36	35
Value for money of office space	26	26
Ease of travelling around within the city	22	25
Availability of office space	22	21
Languages spoken	18	20
Freedom from pollution	11	9
The quality of life for employees	10	10

"Absolutely essential" responses only are included here

---

knowing the buildings' location, were unconsciously deterring
would-be occupiers as they travelled to see the building.
Recognising this problem, mailings and receptions were arranged
specifically for taxi drivers to familiarise them with the locations
and the quality of accommodation.

2. Targeting

Tougher market conditions have concentrated attention in
targeting. This has developed in several ways: a broader
consideration initially of who the targets might be; a switch to
promotional methods which are more focused on specific target
markets; and the tailoring of approaches to individual prospects.

For all types of commercial property in the UK, and for both investors and occupiers, the market has become more international. Nowhere is this more valid than in the London area. Some of the accommodation that has been created in the last 10 years has reflected the need to offer international standards of accommodation and has been promoted accordingly. Broadgate in the City and Canary Wharf are obvious examples and these are already proving instrumental in raising the accommodation standards of developments and redevelopments generally (*see illustration on page 145*).

Obviously, if the targets have become international then so too have the media promoting to them. Property marketing professionals are now becoming familiar with media such as the South China Morning Post and the Straits Times. Brochures and mailing shots are now prepared in more languages, while more visual introductions to markets and schemes, such as videos, disks, and even now the Internet, are being used to generate favourable dispositions across the globe.

The reshaping of the high street is currently prompting retail agents to be similarly imaginative in identifying potential occupiers. One of the forces which will prove really testing is the closure of financial service outlets. Throughout the 1970s and 1980s building societies and, to a lesser extent, banks opened outlets as the population acquired an appetite for financial services. Prior to 1970 finance was rarely discussed in public and, as recently as 1970, only 29% of the adult population had a current bank account. Now almost all have a current account and much else besides. The writing has been on the wall for the high street outlets for some time. The banking mergers of the late 1960s and building society mergers of the 1980s/1990s have left an inherent duplication in many towns. This was hidden as the market was growing. Now that we have reached market saturation, and with advancements in direct and plastic banking, the customer's need for a branch locally is reduced. The high cost base of outlets also inhibits financial services providers from competing more aggressively for customers who are demanding more and more competitive services. It is inevitable that outlets will continue to be closed.

The physical nature of many financial service outlets poses its own problem – many do not readily lend themselves to retail use. A target market that has, however, been identified is the leisure industry. Banking halls in particular can convert into attractive pubs and restaurants, and many deals have been successfully concluded as a result of targeting pub and leisure operators.

There has been a switch in promotional methods, largely away from advertising and brochures and towards direct marketing and presentations. This suggests that it is comparatively easy to identify the potential targets and to make them aware of and understand the project; but more difficult to persuade them to follow through to conviction and purchase. Direct mail and telemarketing can be very cost-effective in generating contact with prospects and their use has become more sophisticated, both in terms of list building and in creativity of approach. They do not, nor should they, replace advertising or brochures but complement them (see Campaign co-ordination below).

Improvements in printing and display techniques have made it feasible to tailor material to individual prospects at a sensible cost. This is not simply a question of flattering the recipient – it means that issues specific to that individual prospect can be included, rendering the communication that much more convincing (see Case study 9: One Park Lane, Hemel Hempstead in Chapter 9).

3. Product Attributes

There has probably been a greater emphasis on the usability of space. Individual target tenants' requirements are considered in more detail and the features of the space tailored to these requirements. More developments are now "shell and core" only and costed accordingly, allowing more to be spent on tailoring. The Broadgate development, for instance, had a separate booklet on the space filling options alone.

The financial benefits are more carefully considered. The Canary Wharf team includes financial analysts who review the current property holdings of potential tenants and are able to structure and present the financial case for moving to Canary Wharf.

4. Expenditure

In keeping with the higher client expectations for the accommodation, so the expenditure on promotion has risen. Budgets of six figures, though not commonplace, are now being seen for larger developments and sometimes much more than this.

Budgets are being set in accordance with the communication tasks to be accomplished. In the case of an existing office building, Adrian Hill, Head of Healey & Baker's Provincial Offices team suggests £75,000 might be a typical promotional budget for a large (10,000 m^2) building. For a new development, however, seeking a pre-letting he reckons "You can add up to a further £200,000 to that". What accounts for the difference is the amount of work that needs to go into creating the Understanding of and Favourable disposition towards the development. With an existing building the product speaks for itself. A prospective or incomplete development needs to be demonstrated with models, drawings, impressions, videos, inter-active screen presentations and so on, in order to reassure potential buyers. All of this adds significantly to the cost.

There is a sense in which such expenditure can be viewed as a basic Finding out process, a test marketing exercise almost. Developments take a lot of money and a lot of time. The time delay can be critical in that a market can turn within that period, as we saw in 1989/90. Even where a developer has researched the market and believes he has identified a demand he may have limited confidence in the market. It may also be the case that he does not have the money to fund the development and cannot get it without a pre-letting in the bag. Either way £ ¼ million is, at worst, a much lower risk and, at best, a comparatively cheap way of securing the pre-letting in order to proceed.

Increased levels of expenditure are being incurred for the additional reason that the market has recognised that a combination of promotional tools in harness is the most effective way to promote (see below). This tends to cost more, but developers and owners are now prepared to spend more because there is a better understanding in the market of what each tool can do and a professional confidence that using them is a sensible investment for the project.

5. Use of media relations

A promotional tool that has become much better recognised and used is that of media relations. One consequence of properties taking longer to let has been the need to maintain profile in the market-place. To do so with advertising would be expensive. It would also, by familiarity, emphasise the impression that the property was still on the market and having to promote hard to attract serious interest. Editorial comment can provide the continuing profile but, by being seen to come from a third party, avoids negative perceptions that might pertain to a lengthy advertising campaign.

Media relations also has the benefit of rapid reaction. Positive stages in a development ofsuccesses in the letting programme can very quickly be conveyed to the market. Similarly, wrong perceptions or criticisms can be countered quickly. By its nature media relations work can be carried out quickly, much quicker than say advertising or brochures. A PR agency can therefore be responsive to developments in the market or the project which makes them so useful over the haul of a project. They can be used to warm up the market pre-launch; launch; maintain interest; boost the price; announce deals; reassure post-purchase; and endorse reputation. An increasing number of large developments and investment sales are using this tool.

6.   Cutting out frivolities   *Freebies*

It is not so long ago that it was commonplace, particularly in the business space market, to offer all manner of "freebies" to viewers and agents alike. These ranged from novelty items to colour televisions to trips. These have substantially disappeared, reflecting the more questioning attitude towards promotional tools used and the greater market maturity.

7.   Signboards

There are compelling reasons why signboards should be an automatic part of any letting campaign. For their physical size and their cost they manage to convey a whole series of messages:

- Draw attention to the property
- Announce availability
- Explain what is available (lease or sale)
- Can give space size
- Advise which agents
- Provide contact telephone

Most leading agents have spent time redesigning their boards, usually coinciding with their own rebranding, to ensure the boards are distinctive and offer the scope for a simple clear message *(see illustrations on page 146-7)*.

Variations in boards can arise at the clients' or local planners' insistence. Clients, particularly developer or redeveloper clients, may prefer to create a specific board that presents their project in a more prominent and co-ordinated way. Considerable creativity and expense has been brought to this area. The Royal Opera House has recently abandoned plans to spend a rumoured £½ million on boards around its redevelopment site. This would have been exceptional but budgets of £15,000 are normal for important schemes, according to Keith Goodwin of Speedway Signs.

In most planning areas, the planning authority has imposed limits to restrict the size of boards. There are standard maximum sizes that are permitted without specific permission. Some authorities, however, have gone even further, ruling against outside boards and the use of colour. This is in stark contrast to other countries, where it seems anything goes. Mackenzie Hill in São Paulo, for example, used a board measuring 600 square metres (6,600 square feet) in 1996.

8. Presentation suites

These probably account for the greatest shift of resource and the greatest advance creatively. Computer-aided presentation has substantially changed what can be presented, the media used to present and the nature of the whole presentation suite.

In the past a suite might have been decorated in materials similar to those to be used in the finished building. Physical examples of the interior finishes would be available, together with artists illustrations and, perhaps, a model of the development. Now a suite will, more likely, be a simple reception room with the focus on a monitor or monitors where prospective clients can view the future development.

Using computer-aided design, the client can walk through the development represented three-dimensionally on screen. This will usually offer an interactive facility. The result is an enhanced realism, enabling clients to picture themselves in the building more readily. Such presentations cost between £50,000 and £100,000 to put together, so they take a large slice of the overall budget. Their value is, however, well recognised. In Central London alone, in October 1996 there were at least 10 developments or buildings utilising such presentational methods.

Presentations have also become portable, with laptops offering the prospect of bringing some of the show suite's capabilities to the client.

9. The Internet

This is still a very recent development and it remains an unproven medium. A number of property organisations are setting up promotional pages and placing property advertisements. In October 1996 the first brochure appeared in its entirety on the Internet, for the Department of Transport's Crowthorne Business Estate (*see illustration on page 148*). At the moment, not enough key decision makers have personal access to the Internet and access can be slow and unreliable. It is early days yet, however, and only time will tell just how significant a promotional tool this will become.

10. Campaign co-ordination

We discussed in Chapter 6 how different promotional tools performed different functions. In a comparatively short space of time the prospective clients do have to be taken through all the stages. It follows that a range of tools will be needed. What is much better appreciated now is the value of co-ordinating the use of the various tools, both in terms of timing and creativity. This ensures that a consistent message is given and that each tool builds on the campaign work that has gone before.

The letting campaign for the Lakeshore office development at Bedfont Lakes, Heathrow, is a good example. The components used were:

- Advertising in trade press
- Simple mailer, for mass mailing

} to build awareness and understanding

- Newsletter, for local community

- Mailshots; –- to prospects in five stages to move from understanding to conviction

- Brochures

- Occupiers Guides, } to move from under-
  with technical information } standing to conviction

- Presentation materials

For a picture of how the various tools can be utilised at different stages of development see Fig. 6, which is adapted from the marketing plan I produced for a mixed use scheme at Kirchberg, Luxembourg.

This better co-ordination also extends to teamwork, with a clear liaison now between marketing agencies, surveyors and clients. Indeed, often surveying firms are now expected to act as procurers and co-ordinators of marketing agencies. To assemble such teams they have had to become more adept at assessing such agencies and working together with them.

Conclusion

This chapter started by considering whether "marketing a building" could really be described as marketing. The judgement was that wherever the opportunity exists to amend the property in response to market needs then it is marketing. Even where the role is reduced to promotion and selling, the practice of marketing skills has now reached a high level. Indeed, marketing buildings is more developed in many respects than the marketing of the companies within the sector.

The next chapter offers a number of recent case studies that exhibit good marketing practice.

Reference

1. Kotler, P, Haider, D.H., Rein, I.,. (©1993)

Marketing Places, BY PHILIP KOTLER, DONALD H. HAIDER, IRVIN REIN.: REPRINTED WITH PERMISSION OF THE FREE PRESS, A DIVISION OF SIMON & SCHUSTER.

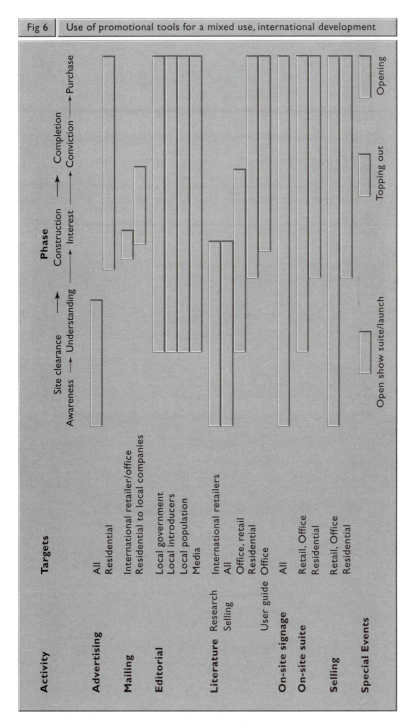

Fig 6 | Use of promotional tools for a mixed use, international development

11. Broadgate and Canary Wharf have taken property marketing to new
levels of sophistication. See page 136.

12. Promotional signage has come a long way over the years –
photographs by courtesy of Speedway Signs. See pages 139-40.

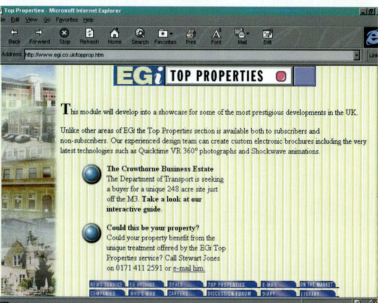

13. The DOT's Crowthorne Estate was the first brochure to appear on the Internet. See page 141.

14. Great Bridgewater's award winning material. See pages 154-5.

15. Brochure for One Park Lane, Hemel Hempstead. See pages 156-7.

16. Minster Court, EC3. See pages 158-160

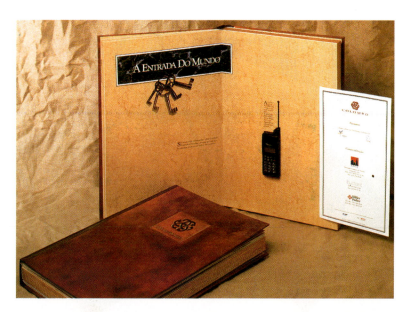

17. The brochure for Colombo, Lisbon. See pages 161-2.

18. Material for Norte Shopping, Oporto. See pages 163-4.

Chapter 9

Excellence in property marketing

This chapter deals exclusively with case studies of property marketing. Each of the examples offered explains the approach adopted and provides the rationale behind the approach.

The studies are all of high profile projects, but projects that had particular markets to address or difficulties to overcome. Between them they offer a mix of property type and a range of location. First, there are three office case studies; one north, one south, one in central London; then two major shopping centre case studies – one covering the domestic marketing campaign, the other the international marketing; and finally, a case study on the building of an identity for a mixed, new town development. The projects are:

- Great Bridgewater, Manchester
- One Park Lane, Hemel Hempstead
- Minster Court, E.C.3
- Colombo, Lisbon
- Norte Shopping, Oporto
- Hampton, Peterborough

Between them the projects have utilised just about every promotional tool in the toolbox, the selection of tools reflecting the specific needs of each project.

Between them too they have won a clutch of awards for marketing excellence.

As ever with case studies, the benefit is unlikely to be derived from a direct replication of the solution adoption. Hopefully, however, they will prompt and broaden thinking as it is applied to fresh situations.

Case study 8: Great Bridgewater, Manchester

This study is of an integrated campaign to let office space.

Client: AMEC Developments
Design: Quest Design
Surveyors: Grimley and Lambert Smith Hampton

This campaign won the St. Martin's Award for the best overall campaign in the UK Property Marketing Awards 1995.

Background

Great Bridgewater is a 20,336 m² (219,000 sq ft) office development in central Manchester. It is the largest office development in the city in more than 30 years and comprises two buildings alongside the new International Concert Hall.

Three of the leading professional firms already in the city – Addleshaw Sons and Latham, Ernst & Young and Price Waterhouse – recognised the importance of the development and, between them, pre-leased two-thirds of the space. The remit was to let the remaining space, which was split between the two buildings.

The development is prestigious and well located, and likely to appeal to major professional firms. Two issues had to be addressed: in keeping with the specification, the asking rents were the highest ever in Manchester; and as the project had been running since 1988 with different interests in the site, there was a need to correct misperceptions in the market.

The solution

A broad mix of promotional tools was used:

— Advertising in local and trade press and in taxis to raise awareness and create a favourable impression of the project;

— On-site illuminated signage;

— Mailing targeted to local professionals;

— A giveaway to the key local targets;

— Brochures, letting and technical;

— An audio-visual presentation of the project's history to invited local targets to correct any misperceptions.

What bound the promotional tools together as an integrated campaign was the creative theme adopted. As the development fronted the same piazza as the new International Concert Hall, the creative theme adopted was operatic. The material used the characteristics of four famous operas to express different aspects of the development, thus:

Madame Butterfly

Faithful to an Ideal. The ideal being the original concept, created by Manchester City Council and the Central Manchester Development Corporation, that culture and commerce could be integrated in one development;

Aida

Designed to Stand the Test of Time. Like the structures of the ancient Egypt of Aida, an architectural statement destined to become part of Manchester's heritage;

Carmen

Buildings Created with Passion. Buildings designed internally with flair and imagination.

I Pagliacci

Part of a Dramatic Transformation. As with transformation of character in the opera, so with the city, as Manchester's vision as a great European city becomes reality.

The adoption of this operatic theme was a potent choice. It was relevant, given the adjacent concert hall; appealed to the professional targets; and provided superb visual imagery for the campaign material (*see illustration on page 149*).

The result

The campaign has established Great Bridgewater as a highly desirable office location. Dibb Lupton Alsop have taken a further 3,500 m2 (39,000 sq ft), leaving just 2,700 m^2 (30,000 sq ft) of the total to let.

Case study 9: One Park Lane, Hemel Hempstead

This study is of a tailored approach to let a headquarters office building.

Client: Scottish Amicable Life Assurance Society
Design: Rob Hawkins
Printing: Syon Printers
Surveyors: Lambert Smith Hampton and Healey & Baker

The brochure for this project won a commendation for printing in the UK Property Marketing Awards 1995. (*see illustration on page 150*)

Background

One Park Lane, Hemel Hempstead is a prime office, headquarters building of 9,300 m² (100,000 sq ft). It is in the heart of Hemel Hempstead, just a few minutes from the M1, and is built to a high specification. The only difficult feature is that, though very well located, for a Head Office the building lacks immediate frontage to a main road.

The building came onto the market in 1991. The initial campaign had run its course, without success in the tough market of the next few years. In 1995 a new approach was devised.

The solution

It was agreed that the likelihood of finding a single occupier for the entire space was limited and that splitting the building offered the best prospects. Larger occupiers, who might take 5,000 – 6,000 m², were coming back into the market. Others were looking for 2/3,000 m² and had already expressed interest, but were reluctant to commit without an anchor tenant.

Given that the building had been available for four years, there was no need to run a broad campaign to generate awareness. The programme devised had two objectives:

— to reawaken interest among agents;

— to move prospective tenants from being aware of the building, to being convinced it could be right for them.

.

For the agents, a competition was launched for them to predict the next deal and the lease terms, which had the effect of re-activating interest.

For prospective tenants, there was a co-ordinated sequence of introductory brochures to raise interest; a technical specification; a computerised presentation in the marketing suite at One Park Lane; and, for interested targets a specially tailored brochure entitled "A Private View". It was this last element that won the commendation.

The team judged that visiting property directors needed something substantial to show their colleagues to help convince them that One Park Lane was the right solution for them. "A Private View", was an expensively bound, high- quality brochure. It used visuals of the building, its interiors and its views to depict what life would be like within the building. Such text as there was, was written in a very straightforward, non-technical way. Many pages were left blank. Text was then written specially for each individual client. Specific interests in, say, communications or educational provision could therefore be incorporated. The required number of copies was then printed as a very limited edition.

The "Private View" concept was thus delivered in a very clear and persuasive way.

Results

The tailored approach has worked. Interest in One Park Lane has been reawakened and a steady stream of interested parties, for both the main and smaller spaces has been generated. At the time of going to press, two offers have already been received.

Case study 10: Minster Court, E.C.3.

This study is of a major redevelopment site in the City.

Client: Prudential Portfolio Managers
Marketing   The Design Practice, Brend Thompsen Shepherd,
agencies: GD & O
Surveyors: Richard Ellis

Background

Prudential determined in 1986 to redevelop a three-acre site on Mincing Lane in the City of London. This represented the largest holding in the City outside Broadgate, which was the principal competition.

Mincing Lane was not a major thoroughfare and one of the main challenges for the redevelopment was to generate a focal point of interest to overcome this.

The existing buildings were to be demolished and the redevelopment to go ahead speculatively, with pre-lets to be sought.

Shaping the product

The location, and the quality of the competing developments, called for a landmark building of striking style. Investment considerations suggested the creation of three different buildings, given the scale of the development. These were grouped around a feature, raised court.

The buildings were to be of different sizes: 9,000 m² (100,000 sq ft); 18,000 m² (200,000 sq ft); and 27,000 m² (300,000 sq ft). With some additional retail and catering, the total space was 59,000 m² (650,000 sq ft). The shapes and floor plates of the three buildings were varied to provide maximum flexibility in letting. Unit sizes were planned from smaller floor plates of 1,000 m² units to the largest of 3,600 m².

The project began with site clearance followed by construction of the scheme in total with the relative sizes of buildings naturally leading to a phased completion programme.

The promotional campaign

The marketing strategy was to seek a pre-letting of either Number 2 (18,000 m²) or 3 (27,000 m²).

The scale of the project, the targets, and the high profile nature of the scheme demanded a heavyweight campaign, both in terms of expenditure and quality of material. The targets were identified from the outset as likely to come from the financial market but, given that the scheme was in the heart of EC3, the insurance market should also be targeted.

The branding of the development as Minster Court and the striking colour logo were derived from its location on Mincing Lane and Dunster Court, which was the entrance to the former buildings. The tools selected to promote Minster Court were:

Advertising

To generate awareness and create a high profile. Media used included The Sunday Times, the Financial Times and the property trade press. This incorporated either photographs of the model, artist's impressions, or photographs of the building, as soon as the project was sufficiently advanced, to demonstrate the striking features of the development;

Brochures

High quality brochures were produced at varying stages throughout the programme, reflecting the progress of the development and the letting successes;

Newsletters

These were produced on a regular basis similarly, and sent to the key targeted financial institutions;

Editorial

This was generated in a variety of national and trade publications;

Site

The identity of Minster Court was applied consistently to the boards on hoardings site;

Show suite

The show suite had three different homes during the course of redevelopment. Initially, it was housed in the original buildings before they were demolished, at which stage it was moved into the livery hall on the adjacent site. It was equipped with videos and 12 interlocking slide projectors portraying an impression of what the finished complex would be like, together with updates of the construction as the project proceeded.

The scheme was also notable for the strong client input into its content. The clients, with both the agents and the designers, ensured that the material was commensurate with the strength of image which needed to be portrayed for both the scheme and its owners.

All told, the promotional costs over a period of about five years amounted to in excess of £1 million, with the advertising alone accounting for £½ million. The power of the advertising, however, generated the necessary awareness and by using dramatic visuals demonstrated the individual and striking character of Minster Court (*see illustration on page 150*). To put this promotional investment in context, the total budget equated to about two weeks' rental.

The result

From the outset, the main targets were the financial institutions and the insurance sector. Approaches were made to key prospects. This generated early success within the insurance sector, the upshot of which is that the largest building, (Number 3) was pre-let to the London Underwriting Centre, housing the world's biggest reinsurers. Lease signing took place in 1990 and the building was occupied in 1993.

This became the draw for letting the other two buildings, 90% of the occupiers of all three buildings being insurance related. Generally, lettings in Number 1 and 2 were in whole floors (either 1,000 m² or 2,000 m²) although some floors in Number 1 were let in small units (100 m² +) to allow for future churn. In practice, the insurance industry within the City shifted as a result, and is now on the axis between the Lloyds building and Minster Court.

Reflecting on an eight-year involvement with the scheme Roger Lister, head of Richard Ellis's City Office, says: "I would not now change, in any way, the product shaping or the image creation. The one thing I would do differently would be to take advantage of the advances in multimedia techniques since then. We tried to convey to potential tenants, in a non-technical way, an impression of what Minster Court would be like to occupy and modern technology can achieve this so much more impressively."

Case study 11: Colombo, Lisbon

Domestic campaign for a regional shopping centre.

Client: Sonae Imobiliária
Agency: Wunderman Cato Johnson
Surveyors: Hillier Parker, In Mont, SPCC

Background

Centro Colombo is set to be the largest shopping centre in the Iberian peninsula, with over 400 shops and a gross lettable area of 122,000 m^2.

Sonae determined on a three-stage campaign to let the space: first to secure the anchor tenants; then to attract approximately 100 "star" retailers; and third, the remaining 300 or so "satellite" retailers (unit shops).

The first stage had been highly successful, attracting the following top international retail names:

Continente	Toys 'R' Us
Warner / Lusomundo	Zara
C&A	Cortefiel
Marks & Spencer	

For the second stage of the leasing programming, Sonae wished to approach 100 leading retailers, Portuguese and international, all based in Portugal. This began in autumn 1995.

The solution

Each of the 100 retailers was readily identifiable by Sonae. The approach selected, therefore, was a direct marketing campaign and Wunderman Cato Johnson were appointed to execute the campaign.

The campaign consisted of an actor, dressed as Christopher Colombus, visiting each retailer in turn and delivering an introduction to Colombo to the chief executive. Sonae telephoned the executives' secretaries in advance to ascertain the executive was available and the actor duly arrived. He was successful in meeting every one of the 100 retailers targeted.

"Christopher Colombus" read from a scroll of parchment that he was introducing the executive to a new world of Colombo. He then left with the executive a lavish personalised brochure.

The brochures were no normal brochures (*see illustration on page 151*). Measuring 61 cm x 42 cm x 8 cm deep (24" x 16" x 3½ " deep) and leather bound to maintain the 15th century look, they embraced modern features within. Visuals of the scheme were included in pop-up format to give a three dimensional effect. Plans had pull-out tags which, when pulled, showed the individual retailer's name on the plans and branding on the façade of a shop in the illustration of shop frontages.

Behind these personalised pages was a mobile telephone (hence the depth of the brochure). This was programmed so that, whatever digits were pressed the executive was linked directly to the Colombo sales suite. On visiting the suite, the telephone could be reprogrammed for general use.

The result

The visiting programme, of course, took a few weeks for the actor to make contact with all of the executives. Of the 100 contacted, 40 telephoned the sales suite and 61 have subsequently taken space in Colombo.

Not surprisingly, given the originality of the campaign, word got round. While the "stars" campaign was still running, other retailers not included in the 100 began to contact Sonae asking to lease a unit in Colombo. By November 1996, with ten months still to go to opening, Colombo was already 84% let.

Commenting on the campaign Alvaro Portela, President of Sonae, says: "With Colombo we are creating a development that, because of its scale and composition, is unique within Portugal. The direct marketing campaign echoed that spirit and helped to create a desire for space which has amply fulfilled our expectations."

This campaign won the EPICA award in Warsaw in January 1996; and the Gold Medal for Business Service using Multimedia in the ECHO worldwide awards in the USA in November 1996.

Case study 12: Norte Shopping, Oporto

International marketing for a regional shopping centre.

This project was the winner of the 1995 Property Marketing Awards of Excellence for the Retail Category.

Background

NorteShopping is a regional shopping centre serving northern Portugal. It is situated on the edge of urbanised Oporto. The developer, Sonae, is the largest financial group in Portugal which has developed and opened one new shopping centre every year since 1989.

NorteShopping, as most of Sonae's projects, has taken an existing Continente food hypermarket which already attracts 12 million shoppers per year, as its primary anchor. There is a core catchment of 1.4 million within a 20-minute drive. These figures indicate that there is an opportunity to create a major regional shopping centre.

Hillier Parker and RKTL, among others, were appointed to advise on the design of a 66,700 m² regional shopping centre. This design provides for a leisure operator and four significant non-food anchors to compliment Continente. The value of the centre is influenced by the covenants of those tenants.

The campaign

It was agreed that the prime requirement was to attract strong anchor tenants, and to delay marketing the other shop units until they were in place. The quality of the anchors influences the interest shown in the unit shops. Therefore it is crucial to attract and sign-up chosen retailers for anchor status.

The need for non-Portuguese anchors was identified. There was therefore a need for the right international marketing material to support the approaches made by the agents/brokers. The Small Back Room were appointed to prepare, within a set budget, all the material to support Hillier Parker in their approaches *(see illustration on page 152).*

The target retailers for the anchors were identified. They had English, Spanish, French or Portuguese as their business language, so the material had to be prepared in these languages.

To achieve the objectives:

*   Major presentations would consist of a boxed set of:

    research report –
    to provide evidence of the attractive retail market available

    brochures –
    to sell the scheme

    separate floor plans

    an appropriate "gift"/reminder of the identity

*   Given the very specific targeting limited to known retailers, and the importance of converting individual prospects, wherever possible material was personalised.

*   The material was consistent across languages with the overprinting of text, wherever possible, kept to one colour.

*   The emotion and status of the marketing material was right for such an important project.

The colours used were indicative of fashion – blue and silver – the material reflected the previous use of the site (textile production). It is intended to install several (made in Oldham) reconditioned textile machines in the mall.

Throughout the design and production processes, material was discussed with the client and their agents. Production was completed in time to launch the project on Sonae's stand at MIPIM in March 1995.

To date, the following anchor tenants have been signed:

Warner/Lusomundo   Zara   Massimo Dutti

The material was designed to help conversations with potential large space users. All the original strategy and communications materials are utilised to their fullest extent, therefore maximising the effectiveness of the budget.

John Rushton
The Small Back Room

Case Study 13: Hampton, Peterborough

An example of a 10-year process where the marketing and image management must be properly planned and controlled.

Background

Hampton is the £1,000 million township being created on a 1000 ha site just south of Peterborough. The township developer, Hanson Land – a subsidiary of Hanson PLC – is creating a quality community for living, working and recreation on land which is being restored to beneficial use following the excavation of clay for brick making. The first time that the name "Hampton" was "heard and seen" was at the 1996 Hanson AGM.

The marketing started long before the first major infrastructure works of spring 1996. The team had been appointed, strategy had been agreed and budgets set.

In the summer of 1995 The Small Back Room, property marketing and graphic design consultants, were commissioned to create an identity which would stand the test of time. It was to be right for all audiences; residents of the four neighbourhoods and the house builders, the commercial occupiers, retailers, joint venture developers, leisure operators, agents across the property spectrum, politicians and press, local and national interest groups. In fact, such a wide audience that it really did have to be 'all things to all men'.

The bigger the project, the more important the project, the longer the project – the more the planning has to be right.

The solution

A graphic symbol has been created which has already been strongly associated with the township.

It is designed to convey a stylish image and a quick impression of life in Hampton – an impression of an environment which combines homes, shopping, recreation and employment facilities as well as water and wildlife. The foreground shows one of the many lakes in Hampton with a pair of swans – the swans being drawn in such a way as to suggest a letter H.

John Rushton of The Small Back Room comments that: "the logo and the associated imagery which goes to make up the corporate identity is being progressed across all material, every item being positioned with its right status, in the right relationship with other items so as to best enhance the brand." With consultants Smye Holland Associates and McLean Aylwin Communications, they are responsible for the "tone of voice" that goes to set the standards of quality expected. The name and the logo are just the central hub of the marketing wheel. The brand building exercise is one of careful control throughout the project.

For example, the commercial opportunities have their own family of literature. Each new site or opportunity does not have its own logo and identity. Because it is clearly part of the whole and shares the same features, advantages and therefore benefits, it is matched together with the rest of the family – which in turn is kept close to the core Hampton brand and likewise to its visual "cousins". These in turn promote other parts of the township and reflect on all commercial products.

Over the next 12 years 5,200 homes will be built for 13,000 people, around 12,000 jobs will be created in offices, factories and warehouses to be built on 165 ha allocated for commercial development, a retail centre will be established with 20,000 m^2 of shopping anchored by a Tesco superstore and a 165 ha country park and 120 ha nature reserve created.

Conclusion

The framework has been set for the visual management of the marketing material. Already there are considerable indications that the implementation is going well, co-ordinated signing is in position, exhibitions are underway, the first homes are under construction, Cygnet Park (the first commercial space) is on the market and Serpentine Green (the shopping centre) is in process.

Research is continual – to track awareness in the local business community, among the people of Peterborough and in the property fraternity. Such continuous measurement of the marketing allows the management of the messages to be effective.

As the project progresses and matures there will be many exciting opportunities to enhance the brand – to provide the perfect example of a new town of such importance – Hampton.

Chapter 10

Summary and conclusions

The book opened with the view that marketing has progressed significantly as a discipline within the sector. This is especially the case with the marketing of projects, i.e. land and buildings. This view was supported in Section II of the book with evidence of recent practice. The one reservation expressed is that the activity cannot strictly be termed "marketing" if there is no process of adjusting the product to match market requirements. All in all though, standards have improved markedly. There is now much highly professional work being applied to the marketing of property projects.

The greater part of this book, however, has been given over to corporate marketing, that is the marketing of companies and their services. This area of marketing is less established and developed within commercial property. The lessons that have patently been learned in the marketing of property are only now being applied to corporate marketing.

Corporate marketing is an inevitably tougher process in that, instead of changing a building or development, the process entails changing management approaches and human behaviour. Hopefully, the first seven chapters of this book will encourage more organisations to embrace the marketing concept and improve their corporate performance.

It is inevitable in this increasingly competitive environment that marketing will become better understood and more rigorously applied. Whether or not it will be seen as marketing is perhaps another matter but, to survive and prosper, organisations will have to respond in an organised way to the requirements of the market.

What's to come?

i.   Market forces

I feel a certain irony whenever I am reminded by property professionals who enjoy quoting Lord Leverhulme, that half of all advertising is wasted, but we don't know which half. This is broadly true — as it is for most communication tools: direct mail with a 99% (or thereabouts) wastage rate; press releases with their 95% wastage rate; sales force effectiveness/agency site visits, etc. The irony in our sector is that property as an asset also has a high wastage element, being in use typically for 2,250 hours of 8,760 hours in a year. One might say the same of most corporate assets: staff, vehicles and so on, but the point is not really relevant. It is where the asset does work that matters. In this regard, it is hard to imagine that British industry will not recognise that it should be devoting more serious attention to its property.

Anybody in the sector constructing a wish list would call for a better understanding of property at boardroom level. It really is an indictment of British industry that so many companies still do not have a strategy for their property within their business plan. I specifically put this question to companies in Healey & Baker's 1995 European Cities Monitor. 26% of the UK's largest companies had no such plan. Having said that they are even so among the best in Europe. The average for all countries was 47%, with Italian (68%) and French and German (54% each) companies the least likely to have a plan. This, however, is also an indictment of the property industry. The task of educating industry is beyond the resources of any one firm to accomplish and would need a concerted promotional effort which ought not to be beyond the capabilities of the sector to arrange.

One of the benefits of generating a broader strategic understanding of property as an asset to be managed for return, like other assets, would be an enhanced appreciation of the service provided by property advisers. This will be a necessary step if that sector wishes to widen its margins, which have been severely eroded in the 1990s. This has in part been generated by the preparedness of some competitors to undertake work with short-term survival in mind, rather than profit. The signs are that market pressures are easing a little, which should reduce such practice. From the client side, price is likely to recede as a determining factor as clients appreciate that good advice impacts on bottom line performance. The best run companies will seek the best service and recognise this must be paid for. Ultimately, too, more clients in the public sector, where some decidedly thin margins have been offered, will recognise that you get what you pay for and will seek value for money. (Value for money is, after all, the basis of selection their Contract Notices say will be used. The problem is that it is easier to recognise cost than value).

Consistent with the greater appreciation of property use will be a greater insistence on research to lessen the risk element of market entry, development, expansion or restructuring. This is merely a continuation of an existing trend, but I do believe research will become the norm preceding developments or company moves.

Given that the sector is coming late to using IT, it does have the opportunity to observe successes and failures in other sectors. This should enable the sector to obtain better solutions to its needs at the first time of asking. One of the biggest constraints for marketing people in service industries is the inability of their organisations' systems to cater for product development. This is not usually the fault of kit or of the IT Department. The failing is generated at the system design stage typically by staff involved in the existing work processes who develop the system to do the job efficiently as it exists then and don't build in the flexibility to allow for future change. This is not an easy issue to resolve since flexibility usually comes at a price and it is not easy to win budget allocation for a resource that might be required at some future stage. Even so the facilities now being developed in the sector should allow for a greater incidence of new service development.

Genuinely new services are inevitably few and far between in any sector, but commercial property has seen few attempts at new products. Increased levels of competition and a closer rapport with clients should dictate that new service development will be a feature of marketing in years to come.

A couple of threats to the sector stem from the notions that in future people will be able to work from home and to shop from home. To date, Healey & Baker's research in these two areas suggests neither practice is as yet very developed. It also suggests there is genuine popular resistance to both notions, particularly working from home. Clearly, however, any growth of such practices would at least change the shape of property required and, potentially, reduce the scope for property activity significantly.

The internationalisation of the market will increase further. Already firms such as Jones Lang Wootton generate half their income outside the UK. Multi-national clients are now expecting consistent levels of service across the globe and the need to control and promise this level of service will prompt stronger global alliances and mergers. Increasingly, too, the staff mix of the largest firms will become more international as more continental Europeans become qualified professional surveyors, thanks to the efforts of the RICS. In turn, more continentals will reach the higher echelons of the leading firms.

This opening up of the market to outsiders will generate a chain reaction, as other sectors have seen. Newcomers bring fresh thinking on the one hand and, on the other, they don't play by the rules. This happened in financial services in the 1970s when foreign banks made great headway in the UK domestic market. Similarly, the Direct Line arrival in the insurance business in the 1980s. What happens is that the sector becomes much more competitive and the old structures of the market and ways of doing business break down. The outcome is a stronger sector, more of a meritocracy, where those players with a clear strategy and professional management win through. Equally there are casualties and I feel this process, which has already started in the sector, will continue.

ii.   Management developments

As corporate clients grow to recognise the importance of managing their property assets, so the level of advice and understanding of their business needs that they expect from their advisers will grow. The larger firms of surveyors have recognised this and set up corporate service arms. The range of skills, though, needed to provide such a service are broader than the traditional surveying skills. Firms will in future therefore recruit more non-surveyors, people with business consultancy skills, to deliver the level of advice required.

In the same vein, a further possibility is the co-operation between different professions. Already we are seeing accountants talking to solicitors about co-operation or merger, as a move towards the multi-disciplinary practice. The same could happen regarding commercial property services.

The enhanced levels of competition and interest from outsiders will inject a stronger urge to manage performance. The whole business planning process, including marketing, is likely to bite harder than it has in the sector to date. This will impact on targeting and on sales force management above all. Because the sales force in most property organisations is intelligent, motivated and runs the business their own performance has often not been managed as rigorously as in most industries. Any opening up of the market to non-traditional players will change this. Targeting and performance measurement have to become more widespread.

Similarly, management will have a clearer understanding of, and demand more of, marketing. As marketing programmes become formulated within the business planning process, so the investment in them will be monitored and assessed.

iii.   Changes in marketing

The greater strategic appreciation of marketing should make the marketing professional's life easier. Even with tougher conditions the market is not usually the problem. Most marketing professionals have agreed with me that most of their problems are internal. It has been my experience over the years and across sectors that whenever a textbook marketing approach is approved by management, without being fudged or compromised, it invariably works.

The call for a greater discipline and co-ordination of marketing activities, particularly as new services are offered or existing services repackaged, is likely to give rise to brand manager type positions where marketing executives become responsible for specific market sectors or for certain service lines. This would be a natural development as marketing matures within the industry.

Market segmentation is another standard marketing approach that is underdeveloped in the sector and must grow. It is true that there are broad divisions within most firms between retail, offices, industrial, hotel and leisure and so on, but these are divisions by type of property, by commodity rather than by client type. Within business space where there is probably most scope for better segmentation there has been little until recently – though some smaller, niche players have exploited this profitably. In due course segmenting the market should be followed by internal restructuring – probably across professional disciplines – into market-related teams.

The greater understanding of what marketing is and why marketing activities are carried out should engender a different attitude to marketing expenditure. Once marketing is seen as an investment and not a cost, and an investment to deliver agreed aims, then construction of the marketing budget and approval for the expenditure should become more straightforward.

In summary, marketing has advanced considerably as a discipline across the sector. Property marketing is now conducted in an increasingly professional way, and it is hard to imagine that, having applied such thinking and techniques successfully to property, there will not now be pressure to rethink the marketing of the companies and services within the sector. The best firms have already started down this track and this willingness to self-analyse and change is truly revolutionary. For the moment, there remains cultural resistance to such progress, but those who do embrace the fundamental concept of being led by the market will be the winners.

Exercise 2: Does your firm understand marketing?

The exercise below offers a quick and simple self-assessment of your organisation's development in marketing terms. Some of the questions are the sorts of issues covered in benchmarking exercises. As with benchmarking, the principal benefit of running through an exercise like this is not what the score comes out at, nor how this might compare with others, but in discussing the issues internally and debating the importance of them.

1. Marketing department involvement in the business plan

A	B	C	D	E
Department helps prepare & put together	Is consulted	Is shown, so as to prepare marketing budget	No involvement	No business plan
❏	❏	❏	❏	❏

2. SWOT analysis

A	B	C	D	E
Done regularly as part of business plan and is communicated	Open discussion occasionally	Top Management only involved	Not done	WOT analysis?
❏	❏	❏	❏	❏

3. Profitability

A	B	C	D	E
Understood and reflected in business plan objective	Established and communicated	Top management knows	Don't know	Glad to get any business
❏	❏	❏	❏	❏

4. Preparation of the marketing budget

A	B	C	D	E
Done with the business plan	Done in response to business plan	Marketing dept proposes	As % +/- on last year	Depends on profits
❏	❏	❏	❏	❏

5. Marketing budget controlled

A	B	C	D	E
Totally by marketing dept	Mostly by marketing dept	Marketing advises others hold	Marketing told what to do	Nobody controls
❏	❏	❏	❏	❏

6. Client research carried out

A	B	C	D	E
Regularly by third party	Occasionally by third party	More than three years ago	Partners do it	Never done
❏	❏	❏	❏	❏

7. Market segmentation

A	B	C	D	E
Marketing initiatives are structured by targeted segments	Some segments are targeted in the plan	Is done on an *ad hoc* basis	No co-ordinated targeting	Our depts are the way we split the market
❏	❏	❏	❏	❏

8. Marketing department involvement in new service development

A	B	C	D	E
Marketing dept drives the process	Marketing dept has a big input	Marketing dept asked to help	Marketing dept only promotes	Marketing dept not involved
❏	❏	❏	❏	❏

9. Service quality

A	B	C	D	E
Standards established + clients' views sought	Staff are trained and reminded	Complaints are responded to. Training is available	Each partner decides	Our Service is fine
❏	❏	❏	❏	❏

10. Marketing staff

A	B	C	D	E
All are professionally qualified and experienced	Most are qualified	A partner is responsible with outside agency help	We have a marketing committee	No marketing
❏	❏	❏	❏	❏

Score 4 for any A box, 3 for B, 2 for C, 1 for D and 0 for E.
If you can honestly score 30 or more your firm does understand marketing.
If you score less than 10, find another firm!
If you score between 10 and 30 tackling these issues will help.

Suggested further reading

I must, over the years, have read dozens of books on marketing. What this has repeatedly brought home to me is that if the reader wishes to understand the concept of marketing without becoming an expert practitioner, then reading one or two books should meet the need and the rest will quickly become repetitive.

I have therefore selected a short list of books that I have found to be straightforward and relevant to people working in commercial property.

Kotler, P. (1980)
Marketing Management: Analysis, Planning and Control
London: Prentice/Hall International.

Probably the single most widely-used marketing textbook on marketing and business management courses. A good all-purpose introduction to the concept.

Enis, B.M., and Cox, K.K., (1977)
Marketing Classics
3rd ed. Boston: Allyn and Bacon Inc.

My personal favourite, this is a marketing person's marketing book. It is an edited compilation of 32 of the most influential, thought-provoking marketing papers written. It is an advanced, not an introductory, look at marketing issues.

Morgan, N.A. (1991)
Professional Services Marketing
London: Butterworth Heinemann.

A lively read, this book looks specifically at marketing within a professional services environment. The author does not pull his punches in criticising what is holding up the acceptance and development of marketing in the professions; and yet, at the same time offers considerable guidance as to how marketing can be implemented successfully.

Kotler, P., Haider, D.H., and Rein, I. (1993)
Marketing Places
London: The Free Press.

This book should appeal to all those seeking to market locations. The book tackles the issues relating to attracting investment, industry and tourism to cities, regions and countries. Although most of the examples offered are North American, they are well chosen and provoke constructive thinking in this still developing but important area.

Index